THE PROSPECT SAYS YES!

A Handbook for Selling Life Insurance

Jim Van Houten,
CLU, ChFC, MSFS, MSM

©2021 by Jim Van Houten

All rights reserved. No portion of this book may be reproduced in any form without permission from the publisher or author, except as permitted by U.S. copyright law. For permissions contact Jim Van Houten at jimvanhouten@yahoo.com.

Printed in the United States of America.

ISBN: 9798732786507

THIS BOOK AND THE CAREER IT REPRESENTS ARE DEDICATED TO THE WOMAN I AM WALKING THROUGH LIFE WITH,

MY BELOVED JEANNEKAY

Many thanks to Jacque Surrett for her diligent editing.

Table of Contents

Introduction 8
ETHICS AND PROFESSIONALISM 10
PROSPECTING 12
    Unseen and Untold is Unsold 12
    Family and Friends 13
    Referrals 16
    Centers of Influence 22
    Public Relations 23
    Cold calls 24
    Orphans 27
    People You Do Business With 30
    Social 31
    Additional thoughts 35
THE APPROACH 41
HANDLING OBJECTIONS TO GRANTING AN APPOINTMENT 44
WHERE TO HAVE INTERVIEWS 48
FACT FINDING 49
HANDLING OBJECTIONS IN THE INTERVIEW 51
CLOSING THE SALE 63
PRESENTATIONS/ SALES IDEAS 69
    Family Needs Analysis 70
    Disability Income 80
    The Three-Point Play 83

Mortgage Life Insurance 86

No Mortgage at Retirement 87

Uninsurable Parents 88

The Guaranteed Foundation Plan 89

The Guaranteed Foundation Plan for Grandchildren 89

Will You Have Enough? 92

Dividend Averaging 92

Conversion of Term Insurance 96

Buy Term and Invest the Difference 101

The Tough Decision 104

Conference Table Approach Talk 106

College Education Funding 109

Special Needs Children 110

BUSINESS INSURANCE 113

How Do You Find Business Owners? 113

How To Approach The Business Owner 114

Ask Disturbing Questions 116

Handling Objections 118

What's Next? 119

BUSINESS INSURANCE SALES IDEAS AND PRESENTATIONS 121

Benefit Stages of a Business 121

Buy-Sell or Business Continuation 123

Key Person Insurance 132

Loan Guarantee Fee 133

Phantom Stock Plan 135

Split-Dollar Plans 137

Golden Handcuffs Executive Compensation 139

Tax Saving Ideas 147

CREATING AND SUSTAINING A SUCCESSFUL BUSINESS 150

Education 150

Policy Production Goal 152

The Goal Card 153

Time Management 156

Sell with Conviction 158

Attitude 159

A FINAL NOTE 161

Building the Bridge for Him 162

About the Author 164

Introduction

I spent my entire working life selling life insurance, disability income insurance, annuities, long-term care policies, and investments. Success required certain skills that were learned through education, experience, and a lot of rejection. Along the way some very fine people shared suggestions, ideas, and advice that helped me. They include the late Jack Nussbaum (a past president of the life underwriter's national association), my father, John Van Houten, CLU, ChFC (my mentor, encourager and guide), my many associates in our agency, my long-time friend, Jack Steinberg, CLU, ChFC (we helped each other grow in the business), and my son, Jameson Van Houten, CFP. My purpose in writing this handbook is to make the reader's path a little easier and a lot more profitable from the information that I share.

This is a very difficult business. There is a lot of rejection. You must have a strong sense of self-worth and a thick skin to handle that much rejection. However, the financial rewards can be outstanding for those who succeed. In baseball, a .200 batter means that 80 percent of the time the batter fails to get a hit. A .300 hitter will be playing in the major leagues and earning millions. That is a difference of one more hit every ten times at bat. In our business, it is the little bit more that can make a big difference in your success. Hopefully, this book will give you that little more that is needed to succeed in a big way.

In the beginning you are in survival mode. You are learning and developing your skills but the successes are few. If you can survive for four years, then you start to turn the corner to easier sales, repeat sales, bigger sales, and more success. You cannot get the big rewards without paying the price of hard work to *survive* those first four years. In our business, I have found that it is very important.

Note: I have herein used the male pronoun for illustration purposes. The prospects, clients and agents could be male or female.

ETHICS AND PROFESSIONALISM

To me, ethics means doing the right thing even if no one would ever know. It is based on the golden rule: do unto others as you would have them do unto you. The Chartered Life Underwriter (CLU) creed follows the same rule.

Professionalism is having the character to apply ethics to all your business relationships even when you could really use a sale. The way you interact with people gives them an indication of your ethics and professionalism. Other people can sense your dedication to being ethical and professional. If you are going to succeed in the long-term, you must grasp the importance of ethics and professionalism.

It is incumbent on you to constantly study and learn. Read all you can. Go to meetings. Listen to the audio recordings of the greats in the business. Take courses and earn the important designations of this business.

I urge you to become a Chartered Life Underwriter (CLU), Chartered Financial Consultant (ChFC) and Masters in Financial Services (MSFS). These are all available from The American College of Financial Services (www.theamericancollege.edu).

A phrase I particularly like to use sums this up for me: **If your goal is to chop down the forest, you are not losing time by sharpening your axe.**

PROSPECTING

Unseen and Untold is Unsold

To make a sale you need people to talk to. This is the first critical skill you must develop. If you have poor skills but a huge supply of prospects, you will still make sales. If you have excellent skills but no prospects, you will fail. With a constant flow of people to see, anyone can sell life insurance. The key is to set up a system of prospecting that never stops and never fails. The purpose of prospecting is to generate names. I did not look for people who wanted to buy life insurance today. I looked for names! My system used all kinds of sources (referrals, friends and acquaintances, orphans, cold calls, public relations, people I did business with, social, etc.) to generate names. The system, if utilized consistently and continually, would generate many names each week.

In my opinion you will struggle in this business until you master the skill of asking for and getting referrals. If you were to rank the various prospecting sources (cold calls, business leads, purchased leads, family, friends, referrals, insurance company provided orphan client leads, neighbors, etc.), where would referrals be? I would bet that referrals are near or at the top of your list. With referrals, they know what you do and they know someone who has done business with you.

In order to get referrals, you need to get people who can refer you and you need to be able to motivate them to refer you. First, let's talk about getting the people who can refer you.

Family and Friends

The most logical place to start prospecting for new clients is with your family and friends. They are most likely to grant you an appointment and will probably listen to your presentation. However, they are also the ones who have known you for many years and have not yet accepted you as a knowledgeable professional in this field. They tend to be hard people to open a case and to close a sale.

I followed my father into the business, so I did not have any family or family friends to sell. My father had sold them all.

I once went to a two-day conference from which I took away only one sentence. It made the whole meeting worthwhile. The sentence was this: **"Do you have any objections to reviewing your insurance program with me?"**

The normal reaction of the public to a question from a salesperson is *no*. Since this question is worded in the negative, the answer you want is a no. After they say no, you immediately ask for a time and date to meet. Always give them a choice: Is Monday or Tuesday better? Is morning or afternoon better? At that point they have to either give you an appointment or admit they did not understand the English language. I have found that this sentence has opened more appointments than any other approach.

When you meet with family or friends, do a complete job. Review their insurance policies. I have found it helpful to get an authorization form signed by the client allowing you to write to their existing life insurance companies to confirm beneficiary arrangements, ascertain cash values and loan amounts, check how dividends are used, etc. Then give them a summary that includes the company name, policy number, death benefit, premium and frequency, beneficiary, guaranteed cash value, cash value of dividends, loans, how long policy will last if it is a term insurance policy, etc. At that time, you can determine if a change of beneficiary is required. Maybe there are loans that can be paid off. Maybe dividends can be used to pay loans or pay premiums or to buy more life insurance. Ask them what the purpose is for each life insurance policy.

Have them request a statement from Social Security. This can be done online. You are looking to see if they overpaid FICA taxes in any year. This also will give them an idea of the benefits payable to dependent children in the event of death, as well as projected retirement benefits.

Ask about their wills and trust. At the very least, they should have a medical power of attorney. With the HIPAA laws restricting access to medical information, each person should have a medical power of attorney, including their children over the age of eighteen.

Do an analysis of their insurance needs. There may be unmet needs to be covered. I will discuss how to do the analysis of insurance needs later in the book.

The real advantages of working with family and friends are that you could be providing financial security for those you love and care about; you could make some sales; and you can have a base for future referrals.

There are people that you know from your previous job. They probably thought well of you, so go back to them to rekindle your relationship. They could be prospects and they certainly can be referrers.

Referrals

As indicated earlier, I believe the best source of prospects and clients is referrals. I have known agents who have the habit so well ingrained that they get referrals even when they are too busy to follow up. In that circumstance, it is best to take on an associate to follow up on your referrals.

A referral is when someone who knows you recommends that you contact a person about business. A referral is more receptive to giving you an appointment because of their relationship to the referrer. "If John Doe thinks you are a good guy, then you must be a good guy."

A referral is more likely to buy from you because his friend bought from you.

The best way to get referrals is to ask. I have found two ways of asking that have been effective. The first is to tell your referrer that you get paid two ways: *"...through purchases you make of insurance products from me and through the introductions you provide to others who might benefit from my advice and service."* The other way is to tell the referrer that he could be making a significant impact on the life of his friends. *I may be the last insurance person they talk to before they die, become disabled or become uninsurable. They would be very grateful to you for the introduction."*

Sometimes, when the referrer hesitates, I will say this: *"If we were at a restaurant and a friend of yours came up to our table, would you introduce me? (Of course) That is all I am looking for... an introduction."*

I was emphasizing getting referrals to one of my agents. He took the message to heart. He called a new client and invited the client's *phone* to lunch... oh and the client could come also. At lunch, he asked for referrals. With the client's permission, he picked up the client's phone and proceeded to go through his contact list with the client. He started at A and ended with Z. The result was fifty-one referrals! Most people have over one hundred names in their phone contact list. That means that the potential is there for over one hundred referrals.

When you first get referrals, your referrer will give you three or more of his B-list referrals and then wait to see how you do. He will keep in reserve his A-list referrals because he does not want to be embarrassed by you to his A-list friends. Knowing that, it is very important that you report back to the referrer what happened with each referral that he gave you. Then ask him for more referrals. Now you will usually get the A-list referrals.

One time, I had a client who was in the hospital for several weeks. After the hospital stay, it would many months before a full recovery. I brought a guest book to him in the hospital and suggested that he have all his visitors sign it. After he was home, I reviewed the guest book with him and he volunteered some quality referrals from that book. That resulted in a lot of disability income sales and some new life insurance clients.

Use a *Who Do You Know* list. It will stimulate names. Ask each question and then wait for a response before going to the next question. Give them time to think of names.

WHO DO YOU KNOW WHO...

Recently got married?

Had a baby or is about to?

Purchased a home?

Changed jobs?

Bought or started a business?

Got a raise or promotion?

Was complaining about income taxes?

Purchased a nice new car?

Sometimes you will get the response that they cannot think of anyone. The reason for this is that they are trying to think of who they know that might want to buy life insurance today. I answer this way: *"If I were selling cars, I am not asking you who wants to buy a car today. I do not know who wants to buy life insurance today and I am in the business. What I do want to know is this..."* (Go to the Who Do You Know list)

Non-buyers can be good referral sources. These are people who have experienced the service and help you provide but they did not buy the life insurance you proposed. They feel badly that you expended the time and effort on their behalf but they did not take your recommendation. Rather than discard them, turn them into referrers. Emotionally, they feel in a less than equal position with you. You helped them but they did not help you. Let them know that you get paid two ways and that they can help you through providing referrals. My experience has been that you can get some excellent referrals from non-buyers. They are very willing to help you. Incidentally, many of those non-buyers will come back to buy from you as their friends buy from you.

There was a time that I was working a referral chain among hospital administrators. One of the referrals was receptive but shared that he was fighting cancer. I reviewed his existing coverage. Then I encouraged him to change jobs to another hospital. In that way, we could convert his current group life insurance into personal coverage. Plus, he would get new coverage from his new employer. He did just that. It increased his coverage by $250,000. He was so appreciative that he became an active referrer. He was responsible for fourteen more sales to administrators for over $1,500,000 of permanent coverage in the next three years. Over the years, he has purchased coverage on himself, his wife, his children, and grandchildren.

Ask for referrals at every annual review with your clients. They will surprise you with more names each time. Take time to drop by your clients' places of business. You will see other people there that may trigger some referrals from your client to co-workers. Even ask for a referral to the client's boss.

Every time I interviewed someone as a potential associate who was moving to my town, I asked them to put together a list of people that they knew in the community they were leaving. Then I had the potential associate contact each person on the list of people and ask if they knew anyone in our community. If the new associate could get at least 100 referrals to people in our community from people back home, then he had a good chance of succeeding. One agent brought over 150 referrals. The third name on his list turned out to be a very wealthy man who needed a lot of life insurance. The agent made MDRT in his first year just off this one referral. In addition, he contacted the referrer back home and sold him.

I have found that it takes four referrals to make a sale.

Centers of Influence

Sometimes it is easier to have someone else prospect for you than to try to do it all by yourself. A center of influence is a person who likes you, likes what you do, wants to help you succeed, and is in a position to be able to refer people to you regularly. People from all walks of life can be developed into effective centers of influence: bankers, lawyers, doctors, real estate agents, contractors, sales representatives, prominent political and/or social figures. Even prospects who do not buy from you may turn out to be excellent centers.

Once you have chosen a particular center of influence, ask him to lunch and show him the kind of work you do. Develop a well-designed brochure with your picture, a list of your accomplishments, and outlining the services you provide in the areas of personal financial planning and business planning. This brochure will serve as an excellent introductory tool that centers of influence can show others. You can use the brochure to remind prospects who you are when you call them back. Thereafter, put your center on a monthly mailing and call back list. Look for articles or ideas to send the center. Call regularly to ask for names of potential prospects. If you make a sale, tell your center. If you did not make a sale, tell your center and explain why. If you have an opportunity to do him a favor in return, do so. This will encourage your center to help you more.

Not only should you keep the center of influence well-informed about your progress in the business but also give him full credit for making contributions to your success. Having a group of centers of influence well-maintained and actively managed will generate prospects that help eliminate the valleys in your business.

Public Relations

Contact the reporters and editors at your local newspaper who cover insurance and financial planning. Write a press release that answers who, what, when, where, why, and how. Include your contact information. Volunteer to do future articles or be available for comments on any stories they may have.

Contact the editors of publications aimed at markets you would like to penetrate. Submit articles about insurance that would be relevant to their readers. For example, I wrote articles for the local CPA society magazine. This opened many doors for me with CPAs for business and referrals. You can do that with the veterinarian association, software association, bar association, electrical contractors, etc.

Volunteer to give speeches at your local Rotary Club, Kiwanis, etc. Contact the program chairperson of the group and ask to be considered for a future program. I found that once I spoke to one Rotary Club it was easier to get invited to other Rotary Clubs in town. Have a good outline of what you will say to share with the program chairperson. This could be disability income needs, long term care, business insurance needs, etc. I also found it was better received if I used visual aids in my presentations. I always handed out some information with my business card attached.

Cold calls

Cold calls are those instances when you approach a stranger seeking an appointment. There is a higher degree of rejection in this activity than other forms of prospecting. If you use it as a supplement, it can be effective. The key is to keep in mind that you are more valuable to them than they are to you. If they are rude, you can walk out. If they are receptive, you have turned a stranger into a friend.

With every new agent I hired, I gave them five hundred business cards and asked them to give them out as fast as they could. If they needed more, we would get more. The whole idea is to get your name and occupation out there.

One effective technique is the "door next door". When you go for an appointment, whether for business or personal, go next door and introduce yourself. Say that you were just next door and noticed their business or home and wanted to introduce yourself. Give them your card and ask if you could set a time to sit down with them and get to know them better.

They may tell you no, but here is the key to turning that around. Say: **"Things have a way of changing. May I call you in ninety days to see if things have changed?"** Usually, they will say okay to get rid of you. They really do not expect a salesperson to keep their word to call back. Then when you call back in ninety days, they are surprised that you remembered and now you are no longer a stranger.

THE PROSPECT SAYS YES!

You are the person who actually kept your word about calling back.

Two stories may help. First, while visiting my parents, they told me of a new neighbor. I went over to the neighbor's house and knocked on the door. When the man answered, I told him who I was, where my parents lived, and I asked to meet with him about his insurance program. His response was to tell me that he was "insurance poor". On my second ninety day call back, he said that he had been waiting for my call. At the interview that followed, he told me that his younger brother had recently died. Upon reviewing his insurance program, I discovered that he only had $5,000 of company provided life insurance. He had a wife and three young children. He bought a lot more life insurance at that first interview.

The second story is about a man to whom I gave my business card. It was a late Friday afternoon of a week in which I was without a sale. The phone rang and it was this man. I did not remember him at first but did not let on that I did not know who he was. His was one of the door next door stops. The prospect's father had died without life insurance leaving his wife in a financial mess. The prospect wanted me to come over right now to set up some life insurance for him. That made my week.

Look for *House for Sale* signs that have *Sold* attached. Contact the real estate agent for the name of the buyers so you can welcome them to the neighborhood. If they moved from out of state, you can ask the new home buyers if you could be their local servicing agent for all their life insurance needs including coverage for their new mortgage.

Look in the newspaper or online for announcements of promotions. Call them and offer them a free cup of coffee if they will meet with you. With a promotion, usually comes a raise. Also ask who took their former position. That person got a promotion and raise but did not make it into the newspaper.

My experience has shown that it takes twenty cold call prospects to make a sale.

Orphans

Orphans are policyholders who do not have an active servicing agent. Do you know what to do about orphans? **Adopt them**. If you are affiliated with a life insurance company, you will find that they have orphans. Ask the agency or company to assign any orphans they can to you. Then go meet the orphans and offer them the service they deserve. Review all their policies including those with other companies. Coordinate the beneficiaries. Do an insurance analysis.

Here is a key prospecting technique with orphans: work the referral chain backwards. If the original selling agent is no longer in the business, find out how they met the agent that sold them. If they were referred, then ask for the name of the referrer. Call on the referrer because they are an orphan also. Remember, the agent for the original orphan is gone, so if he is the agent for the original referrer, then the original referrer is without an agent. Continue working the referral chain backwards as far as it goes.

I worked in an insurance agency office. Periodically, policyholders would call the office seeking service on their policies. I personally met with all the office staff and asked them to refer these policyholders to me. I would provide the policyholders with the service they desired. Policyholders really appreciate personal service. If they were orphans, then I asked to meet with them. If they had an agent with another company, then I asked for referrals and asked if I could add them to my ninety day call back list. They were truly surprised that someone wanted to stay in touch.

An advantage of an orphan is that they are already sold on the insurance company. They are paying money to the company. You are there to counsel and advise them on their next step in building their insurance portfolio.

Please remember this always: **You talk differently to a client than to a prospect.** Instead of selling, you are advising the client on what to buy next. It puts you in a much stronger position. When selling to a prospect, I do not get into an argument about term versus whole life. I sell the term to make them a client. We can talk later about what is the right kind of coverage for the client's situation when I am the client's advisor.

My experience has shown that it takes ten office leads to make a sale.

People You Do Business With

When you pay money to someone, you have the right to ask them for business. Many of the providers I have used over the years (physicians, dentists, repair people, etc.) have become clients. If someone was rude to me, then I found a new provider.

When I was a teenager, my father took me and one of my brothers on a road trip to see the World Series in Los Angeles. As he was exiting a small town on the route, he sped up too soon. He was pulled over by a police officer. He got out of the car and talked to the police officer for half an hour. He even opened the trunk. When he got back in the car, I asked if he got a ticket. Dad said yes. I asked what took so long to get a ticket. He responded that the police officer asked him what he did for a living. My father said that he sold life insurance. The police officer said that he had a new baby and needed to get some life insurance. My father sold him a policy right there on the trunk of the car.

My wife carried my business cards in her purse. Every time she wrote a check or used the credit card, she gave them my card. She would say: "My husband is the best life insurance advisor in the state. You should call him for an appointment to review your program." Then she would tell me who she gave a card to. I would follow up with them within seventy-two hours.

I have found that it takes twenty of these kinds of names to make a sale.

Social

Another effective method of prospecting is what I call social prospecting. There are several ways to approach this, and I recommend that you use them all.

Join your local alumni association. When you go to meetings, pick out a few people that you would like to meet. Introduce yourself to them. Find out where they work and exchange phone numbers with them.

One of the hardest committees to fill with volunteers in any organization is the membership committee. Volunteer for it! The organization will give you names with contact information so you can approach these prospects to join the association. That is a gold mine for you.

Call the potential prospects for the association for an appointment. What do you say to turn the time into a prospecting interview? Ask them about themselves and their work. After talking for a few minutes, the prospect will ask about you and your work. While you are listening to the prospect, listen for areas of interest or special concern. This is your opportunity to probe those areas of interest or just use your approach of: **"Do you have any objections to reviewing your insurance program with me?"** Be sure that you also talk to them about the association and membership benefits.

Join a service club like Civitan, Kiwanis, Rotary, etc. You will meet good like-minded people there. Be sure to get involved in their activities so that you are perceived as primarily concerned with doing good work. Over time half my Civitan Club members became clients.

Get involved in fundraising for a charitable organization. You will meet good people who appreciate a hardworking fellow fundraiser. You may even be invited to join the board after a few years. Some organizations have lists of previous donors to call on. Get all the names you can. It is for a good cause and you will meet new people.

Coach a sports team or be a youth leader in scouting or church. You will meet parents who appreciate the time and effort that you invest in their children. Demonstrate the qualities of good sportsmanship, patience, caring, and leadership. These parents will meet with you after you have proven that you are a person of quality and integrity.

I approached the father of one of the boys on the baseball team I coached. He is a doctor. I used my normal approach with friends. *"Do you have any objections to reviewing your insurance program with me?"* He said okay but assured me that he had a very fine agent. After reviewing his life insurance policies, I asked him who Paula was. He answered that she was his ex-wife. I knew that he was married to Karen for at least four years.

I informed him that the primary beneficiary on all his life insurance was his ex-wife, leaving nothing for Karen. He was shocked and angry. He had told his agent six years ago to change the beneficiary. Immediately, I became his agent. I changed the beneficiaries and sold him more life insurance and disability income insurance. He became a good center of influence for me with other doctors.

Consider joining a trade association. They are always looking for new members. I approached a successful industry's local trade association. I told the director that I would like to join as an associate member. I told her that I believed anyone who makes a living serving this industry should be a member. In addition, I volunteered for the membership committee. They were thrilled to have me join. I received a membership roster! At the meetings, I was the only life insurance person there. I was surrounded by prospects. My name badge said my name and my title as Specialist to the XXX Association, then my company name. Constantly people were asking me who I was and why was I there. I answered that my company developed programs uniquely suited for their industry. I would call them soon for an appointment to talk about what we offer. The association director gave me names and contact information of potential new members to call on. That connection with the industry association opened many doors for me and resulted in many sales.

Go to social parties. When you meet someone and get to know them, look for an opportunity when you can write down their name and information. Then, within a few days, follow up. Invite them to lunch to get to know them better. At lunch, ask them about themselves and their work. Wait for them to ask you about your work. They will. Describe yourself as a life insurance advisor. If asked, "what is an advisor?" tell them that you review clients' programs and make recommendations to enhance coverage, reduce costs, or correct mistakes. Then you ask probing questions and use your approach. This works well with other club or board members.

I have found that it takes six of these leads to make a sale.

Additional thoughts

Sometimes prospects that did not buy insurance from me initially, later did buy when their timing was right. I had to stay in touch or else lose them. Use the two very important sentences mentioned earlier: **"Things have a way of changing. May I call you in ninety days to see if things have?"** Studies have revealed that 58 percent of all salespeople quit completely after a single call on a prospect. Another 20 percent make two calls before giving up, and 7 percent make three calls. The remaining

15 percent make five or more calls. These are the superstars who produce 75 percent of the business.

Difficulties bring out your best qualities if you let them. The superior life insurance sales performance takes place when an individual has a selling philosophy that "it's too early to give up." When things are not going your way, set your jaw, take a deep breath, and try even harder.

A policyholder is not a client until they buy a second policy from you, buy your philosophy, and refer people to you. You will want to focus your energy on converting all policyholders to clients.

I have found that my clients bought life insurance or disability income insurance an average of seven times in their working lives. If you stay in touch with clients, you will be aware of changes in their lives that can lead to a need for additional coverage. Conducting an annual review with clients is a minimum for staying in touch. You may want to talk to your clients more often in the early years of your relationship.

Agents sometimes are tempted by large business insurance sales and they frequently fail when they "jump" into the business market too soon. Concentrate on selling lots of people and eventually some of those people become heads of existing businesses or start their own businesses. Because you have serviced their needs, you will be pulled into the business market.

Having a prospecting system that works for you requires planning, time control, and discipline. You must set up a plan of work activity and stick to it. It is a matter of setting priorities. I constantly asked myself: **What is the most important thing that I can do right now?**

Discipline makes prospecting systems and schedules work. It is not easy to stick to a schedule, to get up early, to work late, to consistently ask for referrals or to make calls; but the agent who has mastered self-discipline can control his future success.

The management of your time is critical to your success. Are you wasting time or using it to further your business? If you waste one hour each day of a work year, it is the equivalent of six weeks unpaid vacation.

Fear, hesitation, indecision, and procrastination are all enemies of time. You need to constantly ask yourself, *am I doing the most important thing I can do right now?*

Prospecting is a daily activity. You need to have a daily goal of setting three appointments in advance every day. I recall the part of the Lord's Prayer that says: "...give us this day our daily bread..." How many times a day do you want to eat? Three? Then you must set three advance appointments every working day. Put up a big sign at your desk of the number **3**. This will require you to set a specific time every day to make phone calls for appointments. This time needs to be sacrosanct. Nothing interferes with your appointment setting. Naturally, you must have a lot of prospects to call. To reinforce this activity, make a deal with yourself or with someone else that involves a reward for making the three advance appointments every day for the week. It may be golf or tennis on Saturday or dinner with your someone special. Having a lot of advance appointments makes you a stronger salesperson, a better closer, and more confident.

You Never Lose!

When you call on a prospect:

One of two things will happen:

That prospect will not be in, in which case you go

on to the next prospect.

Or the prospect is in.

If the prospect is in, one of two things will happen:

The prospect will refuse you an appointment, in which case you will try hard to overcome the objection. You become stronger for the next call. Also, you may make a future call easier.

Or the prospect will grant you an appointment.

If you gain an appointment, one of two things will happen:

You will not arouse interest, in which case you have gained by rehearsing your presentation, and will be stronger for the next appointment.

Or you will arouse interest and make a fine presentation.

If you make a fine presentation, one of two things will happen:

The prospect will turn you down, in which there is a fifty-fifty chance to salvage something on a later appointment.

Or you will make a sale, in which case you have: Earned a nice commission; Increased your renewal commissions for years ahead;   Opened up a new source of prospects.

There you are. You cannot lose. Every call is profit. Every time you see a prospect, no matter what happens, you are a better agent.

It is just a matter of seeing the people and following through!

STP! (See the People)

THE APPROACH

Now you have a name. How do you approach them? I found it comfortable to send a letter or email first. It was important to send the letter or email within seventy-two hours of getting a name. There were two letters or emails that I used. If the name was a referral, then the letter or email said:

> Dear John:
>
> Recently I have been of service to Jim Smith. He thought the ideas I have would be of interest and value to you.
>
> Knowing that you have a busy schedule, I will call you soon for an appointment.
>
> Sincerely,

The letter is short so I could memorize it. When I called for the appointment, he might have said that he does not remember the letter or email. I will then recite it to him from memory. From the letter or email, he knows my business and who referred me. Go right for the alternate close: "Is Monday or Tuesday better for you? Morning or afternoon?"

THE PROSPECT SAYS YES!

Here is what I would say: *"Recently I sent you a letter (email). Do you remember receiving it? When it the best time for us to get together, morning or afternoon?"*

If the letter or email is going to a non-referral, this is how it reads:

> Dear John:
>
> Recently I have been of service to other... (young families, lawyers, engineers, homeowners, etc.). They have found the ideas I have to be of interest and value to them.
>
> Knowing that you have a busy schedule, I will call you soon for an appointment.
>
> Sincerely,

Again, the letter or email lets them know that I will call, what my business is (from the letterhead), and that I help people.

The letter serves two purposes: it gives me a reason to call, and it keeps me on task to make the call. After seventy-two hours, the letter or email loses its effectiveness. Is there special wording in the letter or email? No, only that it is short enough to memorize. Just send letters or emails and follow up.

One time, my secretary apologized for failing to send out the letters for the previous week. I did not know that when I made my phone calls. I got as many appointments as I usually got when the letters were actually sent out. Some of those people said that they remembered the letter (that was not actually sent). The letter is for your benefit to force you to make the calls.

HANDLING OBJECTIONS TO GRANTING AN APPOINTMENT

In my opinion, an objection to granting you an appointment is almost always a smoke screen. How can someone decide that they do not need to meet with you without knowing what it is that you do? Prospects are afraid that you will discover a need that will disturb them and force them to cover that need. Ignorance is bliss. If I do not *know* that I have a problem, then I do not have to spend money to fix it.

Most prospects know two objections. The first one they use is the one that has proven most effective in the past for getting rid of a salesperson. The second one is a weak back-up in case the first one does not work. It is rarely used and they are not as confident about it working. You need to know answers to the four main objections and then you can prevail in obtaining the appointment.

Objections fall into these four categories: No money, no hurry/too busy, no confidence/I have an agent, or no need/ not interested. The wording may vary some, but the general type of the objection is one of these four. In the beginning, when I got an objection that I could not handle, I would go to other more experienced agents and ask them what they would have said in response. After hearing numerous answers, I would make the best answer mine (my way of saying the same thing) and then use it. Practice made perfect.

Here are my suggested answers for each objection category:

No money: *"It is premature of us to be talking about cash outlay until we know if something is needed, how much and why. Some of our clients have actually increased their coverage without an increase in cash outlay. When is the best time of day to meet, morning or afternoon?"*

I am insurance poor: *"Usually when someone tells me that, it means that they wish they had more life insurance but are not sure how to pay for it. Often, poor means that you do not have enough. Shall we get together on Monday or Tuesday?"*

No hurry/too busy: *"I can appreciate the demands that are made on your time, as is true of me. This is why I want to set an appointment so we can focus on the important and urgent. And not let the urgent but unimportant steal your time. The busier our clients are the more they need our guidance. Is it* *better to meet in your office or outside of your office?"*

"No one has a guarantee how long they will be alive or healthy. I could be the last insurance agent you ever talk to. Is the morning or afternoon better for you?"

No confidence in you/I have an agent: *"Oh. Who is your agent? (Pause. Many times, they cannot remember a name) No one has an exclusive on all the ideas that may benefit you. I am sure that your agent would not mind you learning about some new ideas. Is Monday or Tuesday better?"*

I have a brother-in-law in the business. *"How much life insurance were you planning on buying from your brother-in-law in the near future? (None) Then why are we talking about him?"*

No need/not interested: *"I can appreciate that. It is difficult for someone to keep up with their work, their families, and all the potential problems that could happen to them. It will only take a few minutes to find out where I can help you. Would you like to meet at my office or yours?*

"I can understand that. If you had a clear understanding of your needs and the areas where you have too little or no coverage, you would be

calling me. It is my job to make you aware of your present situation and maximize the value of the dollars you spend on insurance. Is ten in the morning or two in the afternoon better for you?"

Sometimes they hesitate or do not say anything for a while, debating in their mind if they should meet with you. When that happens, I respond by saying: **"I am here to solve financial problems for you, not to create new ones."** This has worked well to get the prospects to realize that I am there to help them.

Here is another approach I have used. "Mr. Prospect, the most often voiced fears that people have about their financial future are: Will I live too long, die too soon, or become disabled? Which of these is most important to you now?"

As I mentioned before, consider the objections to an appointment as a smoke screen. Charge right on and get that appointment.

WHERE TO HAVE INTERVIEWS

You can have interviews (not initial meetings) in your office, at the prospect's place of work or home or at a neutral location such as a restaurant. I highly recommend your office. It is an environment that you can control. It saves you time and cost in travel, and it is a small step toward doing business together. If you ask, they will come.

The meetings in the prospect's business can easily be interrupted. You may not have sufficient privacy. Beware of evening meetings in the home. You may become their evening entertainment and find yourself spending three or four hours there. It wears you down as you get tired. I promised my wife that after three years of working evening appointments, I would never have another one. I kept that promise.

Meetings at a neutral location may or may not be good. I recommend that you select places that are not noisy and where you know that you can have privacy. Maintain a list of places that you know are conducive to business.

FACT FINDING

A thorough fact finding is important in handling objections and to making the sale. Knowing all the facts about the prospect saves you from being blindsided in the interview. One time I was in the midst of closing a case when the prospect informed me that he was an heir to a fortune and that if he died, his family would receive a sizeable fortune. I was blindsided and not able to recover the momentum.

Later I learned what to say to handle that objection and actually had another interview with the soon to be client. *"How old are your parents?* (Ages fifty-nine and fifty-eight*) They could live for another thirty or more years. Did your family raise you to be independent or dependent on them?* (Independent*) Then why are we talking about an inheritance that is likely to be thirty-plus years from now? Are you ready to take care of your family?"*

The more information you obtain, the stronger will be your presentation. You will be able to relate to the prospect's actual assets and liabilities. You will be able to identify the areas where coverage is necessary. Here is what I look for:

- Dates of birth of all family members
- List of assets (cash, stocks, bonds, real estate, business interests)
- List of liabilities (credit cards, bank loans, mortgage, other loans—amounts, term of loan, interest rate, payments)
- Potential inheritances
- Additional sources of income (divorce payments, investments)
- Life and disability insurance information (use authorizations to write to other companies)
- Desire to send children to college and anticipated college costs
- Monthly expenses

With all this information, I may be able to help the prospect consolidate loans to reduce the monthly payments and free up money for insurance premiums. I may find dividends in other life insurance policies to help pay for new policies. I may find that the additional income can be reallocated.

The more you know about your prospect, the better chance you have of helping him with his insurance needs.

HANDLING OBJECTIONS IN THE INTERVIEW

An objection during the sales interview must be addressed. Because most prospects and policyholders will have some objections to the purchase of life insurance, it is important for you to know how to handle those objections. Objections can be viewed either as insurmountable obstacles or as tools to help an agent close a sale.

Jack Nussbaum once said to me: **"Selling is telling the truth in an attractive and convincing manner."** I believe selling is an art, involving the proper use of language to convey ideas we wish to share.

The late Frank Sullivan, CLU said: **"Ad lib is for amateurs."** Preparation is vital to the sales process, especially in handling objections. It is important for you to anticipate possible objections and have in mind how to handle them.

I believe that *objections are opportunities*. To some agents, an objection is a huge stumbling block. To me, an objection is a request for more information. An objection offers you an opportunity to present additional features of the program or to clarify features that you already explained but that the prospect does not fully understand.

If the prospect says: "I have to die to win", I respond by telling him that with the policy I am presenting, he will be building cash values that will be available for emergencies, opportunities, or retirement. I give him examples of instances where cash values helped my clients and point out that, in the most recent year, my insurance company paid out more living benefits than death benefits.

I suggest that you commend a prospect who raises an objection for asking an excellent question. I would prefer that the prospect voice his objections now than for him to keep quiet and then say "No" with no explanation why.

Objections give you clues to closing the sale. By listening, you will know what points are important to the prospect, and by properly handling the objections, you can lead the prospect to take positive action.

A prospect can view your handling of objections as persuasion or pressure. You can persuade prospects to accept a different point of view without pressure through the use of examples, further information, documentation or logic. Pressuring a prospect leads to bad relations and early lapses.

The use of stories and examples enables the prospect to see answers to his objections without being involved personally. He can see what happened to other people with objections similar to his and often he learns from the experiences of others without feeling defensive. In addition, stories relax the prospect and shift his attention away from his own objection to what is happening in the story. You don't need to tell the prospect the moral of the story. The prospect will figure that out for himself and in so doing, the prospect will sell himself.

When a prospect wanted to wait before making a decision, I sometimes would share this true story. I was working with three owners of several automobile dealerships. I strongly urged them to enact a buy-sell agreement funded with life insurance. All three agreed to sign the buy-sell agreement that was drafted by their attorney and to purchase the life insurance for the funding. However, one of the owners postponed his medical examination for the life insurance. Before the life insurance could be put in force, he and his wife were killed in a private airplane crash. Not only was the insurance not in force, but the deceased owner had not even signed the buy-sell agreement.

By the deceased's will, his minor children now owned a third of the businesses. A car dealership needs a continuing line of credit from a bank to finance the cars in their inventory with the cars as collateral. The bank asked the guardian for the minor children to sign the bank loans as an owner. The guardian refused. The guardian cannot legally obligate the minor children to debts. The bank called in the loans and removed the cars from the lots. The dealership franchises were cancelled by the auto manufacturer. The resulting chaos forced the businesses into bankruptcy. After relating this story to a prospect, I would ask: *"Would you like to be in business with your partner's minor children? Do you think the deceased business owner thought that he had plenty of time to buy the life insurance?"*

I sometimes said to a prospect who offered an objection: *"Based on the original data presented, I can see why you feel the way you do. However, with this additional information, you may feel differently."* You can lend credibility to your recommendations if you are able to produce more facts and statistics to back up your original statements. Before doing a presentation, you should ask yourself what objections may be raised and prepare ahead of time for them. You may not use the additional information, but it will give you confidence.

Sometimes a discussion of logic will persuade the prospect. Perhaps the prospect raises an objection that he has not thought about all the ramifications of his suggested course of action. By raising questions and logically examining the possible consequences, the prospect often will answer his own objections. A prospect raised an objection during an estate planning interview. The prospect said that he really did not care about saving taxes for his children's benefit. I asked him: *"If the money you could save is not going to your children, to whom is it going to go?"* He thought for a minute and then answered: "The IRS." I then asked him: *"Is that really who you want to inherit your money?"* He thought another minute and then said: "No."

It is important not to get into an argument with the prospect. In arguing, an agent does not introduce new information, he only becomes more assertive about facts he already has presented. This causes the prospect to become more defensive and to close his mind. The agent may win the battle, but he will lose the war. If I get the feeling that an argument could result or that the prospect is closing up, I shift directions and ease tensions by introducing a story.

Here is another way to handle a possible objection. *"It could never happen but suppose you were given a sum of money equal to all the life insurance you own and suppose you decide to quit work and use the money to pay for family expenses. How long could you and the family hold out before more money is needed for family bills?*

No, it could never happen to you, but it happens every day to widows and fatherless children! Don't let your family ever find out what it means to be insurance poor."

I tried to anticipate all possible objections. I sometimes brought up some objections and answered them during the problem setting stage. By bringing up the objections myself, I had the advantage of phrasing them in a manner that was easiest to handle. In addition, I showed the prospect that I had thought about what I was presenting and considered the alternatives.

I had a notebook that I carried with me in which I kept third party material to use in handling objections. For reasons now long since forgotten, I called my book "The Bear Gun". I guess because it was loaded for bear. When appropriate, I would say: *"That is a good question. I thought so too until I read this."* Then, I would open the notebook and let the prospect see the figures for himself. The book contained an answer for objections like: my wife can remarry, God will provide for the family, causes of death statistics for those who think they only die in an accident, a couple of a death claim checks for persons who had their policies for only six months, estate tax table, a sample illustration of a permanent life insurance policy that illustrates the projected cash values, a page I created to show the cost of waiting to buy a policy, an article on inflation and its effects on your purchasing power, an article on the current projected costs of college for both public and private schools, a term insurance plus separate investment versus cash value life insurance illustration I created, an article on wills and trust, and statistics on the causes of disabilities. I recommend that you put together your own notebook of statistics, illustrations, and quotes to use to handle objections.

For example, if the prospect says: *"My wife will remarry."* I would answer by saying: *"I used to think *that also until I saw these statistics.*" Then I showed the prospect a chart that I had previously created from information I had researched. Here it is.

According to actuarial figures from the American Table, the experience of the industry on remarriage of widows after age thirty on a ten year basis is as follows:

Age 30	403 of every 1,000 re-marry
Age 40	193 of every 1,000 re-marry
Age 50	86 of every 1,000 re-marry
Age 60	46 of every 1,000 re-marry

What these figures do not disclose is just what percentage of these women who do remarry have children. However, it is likely that in the case of widows who have young children, there will be difficulty in finding a man who is willing to take on the support of these children. At any rate, it should be noticed that less than 20 percent in the forty and fifty age categories remarry.

A psychologist friend of mine told me that the reason for these statistics is that a widow still loves her deceased husband and is not looking to transfer that love.

I had another page in my Bear Gun that emphasized the importance of starting early to save for retirement. Here it is:

The Value of Starting Early

Two employees saved money for retirement. Joe saved $10,000 a year for five years starting at age twenty-five. He left the money in the account to age sixty-five. Stan saved $10,000 a year for twenty-five years starting at age forty. They both earned 8 percent interest for all years.

Results at age Sixty-five

Joe		Stan
$50,000	Total Deposits	$250,000
$936,789	Total Account Value	$789,544

When you are prepared, anticipate objections and handle them as suggested, closing is much easier. I found that many times, after I have handled a prospect's objections, the close is automatic. I simply said: *"Mr. Prospect, is there any other reason why we should not start this right now?"*

The most frequent objection that you may hear is, "I want to think it over." I recommend that you use the medical close. *"If what we are discussing makes *sense, let's find out if you can qualify."* While the prospect is thinking over the proposal, the insurance company can think over the prospect's insurability.

One of the best experts on handling objections is Roger Zener. He has spoken all over the country on handling objections. He has written books (*Opening the Closed Mind*) and articles for magazines. The MDRT has recordings of his speeches that can be purchased. I highly recommend that you find his books, articles and tapes.

One selling tip I learned from Roger was this:

A selling interview is not a lecture! Many agents lapse into a teaching mode without realizing it. Your goal is not to educate the prospect... it is to MOTIVATE him to take some action.

Prospects are not dumb animals that can be fed endless amounts of facts without any response. Quite the contrary, they will come back at you with thoughts of their own. Often those opinions have the effect of forcing you on the defensive.

An effective technique that can neutralize the prospect's attempt to put you at a disadvantage is to remember the following advice: **When in**

Trouble... Ask a Question! Get the prospect to talk about his situation, his fears, his goals, and his problems. One of the keys to success is helping others see and solve their problems.

In one estate planning case, I was proposing a premium of just above $100,000 for $5,000,000 of life insurance. I was anticipating that the client would object to paying over $100,000 for a policy. I decided to show the premium another way. I divided the annual premium ($100,000) by the insurance benefit ($5,000,000) and got an answer of .02. The premium was approximately 2 percent of the insurance benefit.

In the presentation, I was asked what the premium is. I answered that it is 2% of the insurance benefit. *"You would have to pay in premiums for fifty years to put in as much as your family is guaranteed to get back!"* The prospect said yes!

Suppose the prospect said to you, "I like this program and would like to start it in a few years once we get ABC paid off." Another page I had in the Bear Gun was The Cost of Waiting.

This was very effective in explaining the real cost of waiting to start a policy. The differences in projected gains were substantial compared to the savings in premiums by postponing a policy for five years or ten years. On this page, I had columns for ages thirty, thirty-five, forty, forty-five, and fifty. Under each age, I listed the annual premium for $250,000 of whole life insurance so the client could easily see how the premium increased with the age at which the policy was purchased. Below each age and premium, I listed the projected cash values at ten years, twenty years and at age sixty-five. Then I had the total of all premiums paid to age sixty-five.

Subtracting the total premiums from the total cash values at age sixty-five gave me a projected gain number. I would show the prospect how much the gain dropped by waiting to start the policy five years or ten years from now. (The page had to have a number of disclaimers relating to using non-guaranteed projections.) I found this page to be very effective with those who would like to procrastinate.

One hint: when showing a policy illustration to a physician or dentist, refer to the illustration as an *x-ray* of a policy. To a contractor or architect, it is a *blueprint* of a policy.

Look for creative ways to subtly use their business terminology in your presentations.

CLOSING THE SALE

It has been said that you are closing the sale throughout the interview. In the close, you will want to summarize those items that your client indicated were important to him, tell him that you will take care of the details, and then ask him to take a small action step, such as "sign here" or arrange the medical exam time and date.

I have found that the more cases you have open the better closer you will be. If you have few open cases, you will tend to treat the prospect with kid gloves and will not want to upset him. The prospect may perceive this as weakness on your part and that you are more concerned with making a commission than helping him. If you have many open cases, you can be stronger and more affirmative. The prospect will perceive that you are more concerned with helping him than making a commission. I have even said to a prospect: *"You need this insurance much more than I need a sale."*

I have found the Waiver of Premium close to work well. It involves describing the Waiver of Premium rider and how it waives premiums if the insured becomes totally disabled for as long as six months.

The cash values continue to grow and the insurance coverage continues without paying premiums during the disability. *"If you became totally disabled, what would happen to your life insurance? Is there someone who could pay the premiums for you? You certainly would not want to let the policy go. With the Waiver of Premium rider, the life insurance company will waive the premiums if you qualify. You must be totally disabled for at least six months. Once approved, the company will refund all premiums paid during the six months waiting period. They will continue to pay the premiums until recovery. And the best part is that the cash values will continue to grow as if you were actually paying the premiums. Do you want to include that rider in your coverage?"*

Then mark his response on the application and keeping asking questions.

The beneficiary close works the same. You ask and discuss how the beneficiaries should be set up. Then record the decision on the application and continue completing the forms. If married, the insured will usually name his spouse as primary beneficiary. Next, ask if the children should be named contingent beneficiaries. If the children are minors, recommend that a guardian be named to administer the proceeds on behalf of the minor children until they become of age.

Here is another possible close. *"I think I can understand your reason for hesitating. Your retirement days are actually a long way off and certainly death or a crippling disabling illness does not seem imminent at this time. However, the possibility of death or disability is not all that gives urgency to starting this plan. This plan is only available to those who are in good health. Yet today's health is no guarantee of insurability tomorrow. Every day people slip across the line of un-insurability, often without even knowing it, because you do not have to be really sick or disabled to be uninsurable. Today there are no IFs about this plan, but delay will create two big IFs for tomorrow - If you are alive and If you are insurable.*

Let's put this plan into effect for you today. You will always be glad that you did, and we will eliminate the possibility of you being sorry that you did not. Shall we arrange for you to pay the premiums annually or would installments be more convenient for you?

Mr. Prospect, I think that too frequently, we talk about the things that a man should do for his family without also pointing out just what the benefits will be for him. I am sure you and I agree that this would be a fine plan for your family to have if you should die. However, the wonderful thing about this cash value life insurance policy is that you cannot be good to your family without also being good to you. Through this plan you are sending dollars to wait for you with valuable retirement income benefits. But these dollars will not be waiting for you unless you start sending them ahead now. Let's start sending these dollars ahead today. You will be glad that you did. What is your date of birth again?"

Another way to close is to ask the client to make the check out to XYZ Insurance Company. *"I want to get the insurance company on the hook as soon as possible. You do have a ten day free look if you change your mind,"*

He wants to think it over. *"What do you want to think over? Let's look at the insurance benefit again. Let's look at the premium and cash values."* Go to the bathroom for a few minutes to give him time to look it over. You want him to make a decision while everything is fresh in his mind. If you do leave, call him back the next morning, not next week.

No one has extra money. Allocating money is a

matter of priorities. Does he want it more than something else? You need to make him realize he needs it and wants it.

When you ask a closing question, it is imperative that you remain quiet. The next person to speak has to be the client. If you speak, you lose. You asked the closing question. Wait for the answer. I have seen many sales lost when the agent could not stand the silence and had to say something more. The momentum was lost.

I have seen statistics that show that 90 percent of sales are closed in the first closing interview. A closing interview is when one specifically asks the prospect to buy. It may involve completing the application or writing a check. Another 5 percent is closed in the second closing interview. So do a good job the first time.

When you have a second interview, it is important to review and re-sell what was covered in the previous interview(s). After you leave a prospect, his interest in what you covered starts receding. The old-fashioned water pumps required you to pump vigorously and finally water would flow. If you stopped pumping, the water would recede back down the pipe. To get more water, you had to start pumping hard all over again. In the same way, you must re-sell the key points of the previous interview to get the interest and commitment level back up.

One idea I learned from Roger Zener was how to get the big premium paid annually instead of monthly. *"John, are you the type of person who after paying the life insurance premium wants to celebrate with his spouse or are you the type of person who wants to throw up? Well, do you want to throw up once a year or twelve times a year?"*

Roger got more than a few six-figure annual premiums with this.

PRESENTATIONS/ SALES IDEAS

Everyone who knows me will attest that I was always sharing sales ideas in every meeting that I conducted. This next section will include presentations that can be used to solve a variety of needs. I will first address sales ideas for individuals then progress to sales ideas for businesses. These ideas and presentations have been field-tested and proven very effective. Feel free to modify the wording to fit your personality. If you change too much, you will lose effectiveness.

When I was quite new to the business, a veteran agent took me into an office and closed the door. He then said the following to me. "When you graduate from carpenter school and go to your job site, the first thing that happens is that the master carpenter comes over and says: boy, this is a hammer. That is the only tool I want to see you with. When you are so good with the hammer that you can hammer with your right hand or your left hand, forward or backwards, and upside down, then and only then will I give you a saw. When you see a nail, you don't saw it. You use a hammer. When you are so good with the saw that you can saw with your right hand or your left hand, forward or backwards, upside down, then we will go on to the next tool." At that point, the veteran agent got up and left.

I sat there stunned for a while. Then I realized what the story was telling me. I had to become an expert in using one presentation before I moved on to the next presentation. Rather than being a "jack of all trades and a master of none", I became a master of each presentation. That is what you will need to do. Master each presentation before moving on to the next, unless a situation dictates a particular presentation be used.

Family Needs Analysis

This presentation is to do an analysis of a family's assets, income, debts, and needs. This analysis should be done periodically as a family's circumstances will change. This review is particularly important if the family should move, have a new family member, change jobs, receive an inheritance, or pay off debts. This type of analysis involves software for the computations but I am proposing a different type of presentation than going over a computer printout.

A family needs analysis is really combining several needs in one presentation. To be effective, each need must be "sold" and committed to by the family. The needs are: final expenses, debts, mortgage, family income, and educations. Let's look at each one individually.

Final expenses include burial or cremation costs, burial plot, medical costs, funeral expenses, and perhaps additional expenses assisting family members to be able to attend the funeral or memorial service. *"Do you want to be buried or cremated? How much do you think it might cost for all final expenses?"* Guide them to allocate at least $10,000 for this need.

Most families have debts. These include school loans, credit cards, car loans, title loans, or bank loans. Ask for details on all loans. What is the principal still owed, the interest rate, the monthly payment, and the term of the loan? *"You came into this world debt free. Does it make sense to you that you should leave the same way? How much is needed to pay all your debts?"* By the way, you may be able to recommend a consolidation of loans and free up some monthly cash flow for premiums. It would pay you to develop a banking connection to be able to recommend clients for consolidation loans.

One of the largest purchases a family makes is a home. Most everyone has a mortgage. The payment can be sizeable for any family. With the loss of one parent, the monthly payment can be overwhelming. The home offers an emotional anchor to weather the storm of dealing with the loss of a loved one. *"The loss of you or your spouse is going to create a sizeable financial burden for the survivor. The monthly mortgage payment may be more than you can handle. The loss of a parent is a tremendous emotional impact on your children. To lose their house and move will create even more emotional turmoil for the children. They need an anchor, their house, in this storm. Do you want the mortgage paid off when you die? Is this important to you? How much is it?"*

Family income is the replacement of the income when someone dies. No doubt that income is necessary for the financial well-being of the family. Most dual income families need both incomes even if there is not a mortgage payment to make. Social Security provides an income as long as there are minor children. A computer analysis will calculate the present value of the lost income and factor in the payments from Social Security.

One important consideration in determining family income need is that, for the benefit of minor children, it may be of great value to have the surviving parent spend more time home with the children. Maybe the surviving spouse could work while the children are at school and be home when they are. Statistics prove that most juvenile delinquency occurs after school or in the summer when parents are not home. In a dual income family, do the analysis both ways since we do not know who will die first.

"One of the finest gifts you can give your spouse is the option of being a fulltime parent or working on her schedule. Instead of being forced to work perhaps in a job she does not like, you have given her the freedom to choose whether she will work and where. Will she have to remarry? The statistics are that second marriages with minor children involved fail over 70 percent of the time. This means more heartache for the children. One of the finest gifts you can leave your children is a fulltime parent. Is this important to you? To make that possible how much monthly income will be required to support

your family? Is this after paying off the mortgage or with a mortgage payment included?"

Education is another important need. It has been proven that the higher the education level, the higher the income. If it is important to the family to provide college educations for the children, then this is an important need to cover.

Is the funding for a private college or public? I suggest that you research costs in your area for private and public colleges. What funds already exist for this purpose? Will grandparents be helping? *"Is it important to you that college educations be provided for your children? How much will that cost?"*

Now do the calculations on the computer to come up with the total life insurance needed. Then put your presentation together showing several life insurance solutions.

If you offer at least two choices of insurance plans, then the client is focused on which one to choose. If you offer only one choice, then the client is focused on yes or no.

If the client objects to your solution as too much insurance, then say: *"This is what you need to cover your family's needs. Tell me what you want to eliminate: educations or income for the family? You said that these were all important to you. Can you really afford to deny this coverage to them?"*

Have you ever proposed life insurance to a prospect and he said, "I have to talk to my spouse"? Then in the next day or two you follow up and were told that "my spouse said no". How did that happen? Probably it went something like this.

Prospect: "I met with John Q. Agent today." Spouse: "What did he want?"

Prospect: "He thinks we should increase our life insurance." Spouse: "Before we spend money on that, I would like to get a new washer, a new car, and a vacation. The kids need new clothes."

There goes your sale. The need may be there, but the motivation is totally lost. Ideally, you want to talk to both spouses at the same time. However, if you cannot talk to both spouses, then it is imperative that you use a presentation letter so that the spouse will get the same information and motivation that the prospect heard.

This idea was first developed by Jack Nussbaum. Here is an example of the presentation letter.

THE PROSPECT SAYS YES!

Dear _____:

It was a pleasure to visit with you and exchange ideas with reference to your life insurance estate.

As I see it, your present concern is to arrange your life insurance so (name of spouse and children) can be assured a livable income in the event of your early demise.

You have proven that you have the ability and have created an opportunity for yourself. Given sufficient time, it is clearly seen that you will go a long way towards establishing happiness and prosperity for your family. The only cloud on the horizon is the question of time. Will you have enough time to reach your goals? The practical solution to that question is through the use of a properly arranged life insurance estate.

The following life insurance estate will carry out the objectives that your present environment and standard of living require.

It will guarantee to (name of spouse and children) a comfortable, livable income without the necessity of investment worries. They will never be dependent on anyone for either financial aid or advice.

Whenever this may become a claim, the following payments will be made:

> Immediate Cash to (name of spouse)
> $_____

(For last expenses, burial costs, last sickness, pay all debts including credit cards, current bills, and set up an emergency fund.) (Any interest earned to be paid out on December 15th each year as a Christmas present from you.)

> To Pay Off the Mortgage $_____

(Or it can be used to purchase another home if (name of spouse) decides to move. Either way, your family's housing is guaranteed.)

To Help Provide a College Education

> for (names of children) $_____

(Funds to be invested conservatively until needed. If one of your children decides not to go to college, then their share can be paid out at age twenty-five.)

> Monthly Income to (name of spouse)
> $_____

(A guarantee of financial freedom and the ability to have choices)

Total Paid Out (including Social Security):
$_____

Additional Life Insurance Required:
$_____

The proper type of life insurance does a double duty. It takes care of your family if you die too soon and will take care of you and (name of spouse) if you live too long. My recommendation is that you own as much permanent life insurance as you possibly can. Your needs for life insurance protection are just beginning and will probably be increasing. These needs may last for many years to come. At the same time, you will be building a valuable cash reserve fund for emergencies or real business opportunities.

This is very simple for me to say, but I want you to know that I realize we cannot do everything we want to do when we want to do it. For that reason, I suggest that when you cannot own immediate permanent life insurance, you buy level term life insurance which can be converted over a period of time to sound, permanent life insurance. As your income increases and your standard of living becomes more costly, you can rearrange your life insurance to suit your needs at that time.

It is my sincere recommendation that you consider and choose one of the following plans:

$_____ of permanent life insurance requires a premium of $_____ a year ($_____ monthly). Please look on the attached illustration for projected cash values. Cash value figures include illustrative dividends based on current dividend schedule, not guaranteed.

$_____ of permanent life insurance with $_____ of level term life insurance requires a premium of $_____ a year ($_____) monthly).

$_____ of level term insurance requires a premium of $_____ a year ($_____ monthly).

Each plan will provide the necessary life insurance protection for your family. Plan 1 or Plan 2 will build a cash reserve for the educations of your children or for retirement.

It is my professional opinion that the ideas expressed herein are sound and should be carried out immediately.

Sincerely,

This method of presentation has proven very effective by me and many other agents. A computer-generated presentation often misses the motivation and seems impersonal. Not only does this approach get the prospect the coverage needed, it sets up the ability to discuss conversion of term insurance in the future.

Disability Income

The ability to generate an income through our work often defines us. As long as we have our incomes, we can pay off debts, meet living expenses and save for the future. Loss of the ability to work can cause bills to fall behind, assets to be sold off, and perhaps bankruptcy. In recent years, disability has been the most often cause quoted in bankruptcy filings.

Most people do not have disability income insurance. Many employers have discontinued this type of coverage. The definition of disability under Social Security makes it very difficult for someone to obtain. Single people are particularly vulnerable because they do not have a spouse to help out.

Every one of your clients should have disability income insurance.

"You have insurance that covers your home and your cars. But do you have insurance on your biggest asset? Your biggest asset is your income. If you multiply your income times the remaining number of years of work, you will find that it is your biggest asset. If you were to become disabled due to an accident or illness, how would you replace that asset? How would you pay your bills which now would include medical bills?

If you think things can be tight now while you are working, imagine how tight it will be without your income. What disability income coverage do you have?"

Here is my written presentation for this need.

The most valuable asset you have is the ability to generate an income. It is your earning power that is needed to meet your personal and family needs, and in many cases, your business needs. This means that a long-term disability can derail your plans and cause you severe financial hardship.

Of all disabilities only 13.4 percent were due to injury. Sicknesses account for 86.6 percent.

In evaluating the importance of this risk to you, you should ask yourself:

How much of your income goes to paying daily living expenses? If you are too sick or injured to work, how much income do you have guaranteed from other sources? What must you and your family give up to survive financially?

It is realistic that your savings and investments will disappear. It may not be reasonable to expect that your spouse will work if he or she must assume care-giving responsibilities.

The solution to this potential threat to your financial independence is to have adequate disability income insurance. The properly designed program will provide financial peace of mind.

Attached is an illustration of disability income insurance that covers both total and partial disabilities. The premium is guaranteed level. The benefits are paid to you tax free. The definitions are very favorable.

This is a major deficiency in the protection for your family. This insurance should be implemented immediately.

The Three-Point Play

The "three-point play" involves planning for three possible financial problem points in life—disability, death, and retirement. This method helped me repeatedly sell two or more policies every time I closed and the closing was successful over 90 percent of the time.

The "three-point play" has flexibility in that it can start at any of three points. You can start first with the consideration of retirement, relate it to permanent life insurance, then go to disability income insurance. Or you could start with permanent life insurance and go on to the other two. The whole idea is to first capitalize on the income level needed to sustain the client's family, then to realize that this income must be insured against disability and premature death, and must be set aside to provide for comfortable retirement years.

In explaining the importance of protecting income against disability, I use the analogy of the goose that laid the golden eggs. "Which is more important...the goose or her eggs? Most people insure their golden eggs—automobiles, homes, *jewelry, furniture, etc. Those are some of the material things which can be purchased with our income, but even if those material possessions are not insured and we should lose them, as long as our income continues, we can always replace them. Income is really the goose that lays the golden eggs and without that income none of the other possessions would be possible. As long as the income keeps coming in, we are in relatively good shape. But if the income stops, most people would not be able to even pay the insurance premiums covering their possessions. Being realistic, having insurance on the goose is the most important insurance of all. Without her, there would soon be nothing."*

After emphasizing the importance of disability income insurance, you then proceed to determine the extent of coverage the prospect needs. This involves an analysis of his income and expenditures. You also need to know about unearned income, assets, and liabilities. You need to find out the present premiums for life insurance and contributions to retirement.

This is where the three-point play comes in. You will point out to the prospect that his earned income is subject to three risks—disability, retirement or death—and that the protection of his earned income is complete only when he has insured against each one of these possibilities. Capitalizing on the disability income insurance need you established earlier, you will point out to the prospect that the present value of his future earnings is equal to the amount of loss his family would suffer if he should die prematurely, and that amount represents his present life insurance need plus the amounts needed for debts, mortgage, and educations. Focusing again on the prospect's earned income, you then discuss retirement.

Prospects readily agree that their retirement income needs are based on the standard of living their present income affords them and that preservation of as much of this income as possible, after retirement, is desirable. Using that as a base, you can determine the amount of money the prospect needs to have at age sixty-six in order to provide monthly payments equal to his retirement needs. The cash values of the life insurance can be shown to help meet this need.

It all fits together into one neat package and it makes sense to the prospect. The needs for disability income protection, life insurance, and retirement can all be related to present earnings.

As the client's earned income rises, you will have to reevaluate how much disability income insurance he will need. This leads to re-evaluating how much life insurance is needed to replace the income for the family and how much more to set aside for retirement to meet this new level of income. It is a constant upgrading process. At this point, you are not selling; you are advising your client.

This approach to problem solving has been very effective with professionals, business owners, and wealthier prospects.

Mortgage Life Insurance

"As a homeowner, you know that the people who lent you the money to enable you to buy your home require that there always be fire insurance on the house to protect them. That, you will agree, is a sensible, business-like requirement by the lender.

But the reason that so many people own mortgage life insurance is that they know it is far more likely that they will "burn down" rather than that their homes will catch fire. The mortgage company has their protection. Mortgage life insurance is your family's protection.

For every fire loss suffered during the period of the average mortgage, there are sixteen deaths among the borrowers,

Mr. Prospect, your real hazard is not fire!"

No Mortgage at Retirement

Most people want to cover their mortgage in the event of a premature death, so they buy term insurance in that amount. Then they upgrade their home and acquire a bigger mortgage. This leads to a new term insurance policy. They will probably move several more times. With age comes higher life insurance premiums for these new policies.

Some people desire to pay off their mortgage early and save a lot of interest. This is done with additional principal payments every month. While this will save some interest, this additional money paid in is not easily accessible for emergencies or opportunities. There is a better way.

Consider buying a cash value life insurance policy with an increasing death benefit. Over time, you will build cash values and the death benefit will grow. Currently, the interest rate you earn on a policy may be greater than the interest rate you pay on your mortgage. You will keep this policy and add to it as needed. At or before retirement, most people downsize. By then the cash values may be enough to pay off the mortgage and allow you to enjoy your home in retirement debt free.

Uninsurable Parents

Occasionally, you will find a parent who is absolutely uninsurable. Talk to him about life insurance for his children. A policy on his children can have an insurability protection rider that allows the insured to increase coverage up to eight times over a twenty-year period of time without evidence of insurability. Each company's rider may vary.

When my brother developed cancer at age twenty-eight, we used this rider to increase his coverage four more times. I had asthma early in my working life that would have increased my premium for new coverage. Instead, I used my options until my asthma was under control.

The Guaranteed Foundation Plan

This is an idea to share with grandparents to benefit their grandchildren. Once you start one of these plans you will be selling more policies as more grandchildren come along. Here is the presentation and the approach letter.

The Guaranteed Foundation Plan for Grandchildren

The purpose of this Plan is to provide a guaranteed financial foundation for the future of a grandchild. Usually, parents are focused on meeting the current needs of their families. It is the grandparents who are able to provide the resources to help their grandchildren get a financial head start. Features of the Plan:

- It is a cash value life insurance policy from a highly rated life insurance company.
- The policy builds guaranteed cash values.
- It earns guaranteed interest.

- The policy receives annual dividends which will be reinvested.
- Policy is paid up at the insured's age sixty-five.
- The life insurance benefit is guaranteed and increases with dividends.
- There is a rider that guarantees the insured eight (8) opportunities to increase the insurance coverage without having to take a physical exam. This will be advantageous when he/she has a family.
- Details of the Plan:
- Ownership. The owner of the Plan is decided by the purchaser. It could be the grandparents or the parents. At some point in adulthood, ownership can be transferred to the insured.
- Beneficiary. Initially the beneficiary will be the owner. Later this could be changed to someone else (spouse, children, etc.).
- Premium. Depends upon the age of the grandchild. Once established, the premium remains fixed. The larger the premium, the

higher the cash values. For the grandchild, this premium emphasizes the importance of regular and consistent savings.

Dear (grandparent name):

Of all the gifts you give to your grandchildren, most will be lost, broken or discarded. Farsighted grandparents search for gifts that will last and help their grandchildren secure a stronger foundation for the future.

Attached is a description of such a gift. "The Guaranteed Foundation Plan for Grandchildren" will last for your grandchildren's lifetimes. It increases in value over the years. It helps teach the lessons of thrift and consistent savings. You can give them a financial head start with guarantees.

Please review this Plan. Then please let me know if you would like to learn more or to start such a Plan for your grandchildren.

I look forward to hearing from you.

Sincerely,

This has been very well received and successful in generating a lot of sales. In addition, as you are completing forms on the grandchildren, it gives you the opportunity to talk to the parents.

Will You Have Enough?

FORTUNES FLOW THROUGH YOUR HANDS...BUT HOW MUCH HAVE YOU **KEPT** SO FAR?

You are _____ years old.

You have worked hard for _____ years.

Your total earnings for that period were $_____.

You have $_____ left to show for your work.

What will you do now to make your future different?

Dividend Averaging

Many people have several whole life policies that pay dividends. There are many fine life insurance companies like MassMutual, Northwestern Mutual,

New York Life, etc. that have been paying dividends on their whole life policies for many decades, some over one hundred years. These dividends usually are re-invested in the policies in the form of paid-up additional insurance (paid-up additions) or accumulations. The concept of dividend averaging is to use the annual and accrued dividends from existing policies to purchase a new policy. It is not unusual to be able to add another policy for 20 - 40 percent more coverage.

You would first seek a past history of dividends to get a feel for the stability of the past dividends and then get a projection of future dividends for each policy. Add up the current annual dividends and add 20 percent of the accrued dividends to ascertain the premium amount available for the purchase of the new policy. Have the new policy's dividends be applied to reduce the new policy's premium.

The presentation to the client would be like this: *"If I could show a way to add 20 - 40 percent more life insurance coverage on your whole life policies without any cash outlay from your pocket, would be willing to take the additional coverage?"*

The objection he could raise is that the cash values

of his existing policies would be reduced by the dividends withdrawn. You would answer that the new policy is also building cash values with those dividends while you are benefiting from more insurance coverage.

How is this done once the policy is sold? The initial premium is paid by withdrawal of some accrued dividends. Next year and thereafter, when the premium notice is received, the client or you will contact the company or companies to request that a check be sent from accrued dividends for the amount of the premium due. Or, you can change the dividend option on the existing policies to have the dividends paid in cash to the client. Upon receipt, the client would deposit these checks in a special insurance savings account to await the premium due date. If more is needed, then contact the existing insurance companies for some more accrued dividends. If the new coverage is with the same company as the existing policies, this can usually be set up internally to have the dividends automatically transferred from existing policies to the new policy to pay the premium due.

It is helpful to you to have a prepared authorization form signed by the client to his various insurance companies to be able to obtain policy information, policy illustrations, and needed forms. The form that I used was this:

_____ 20__

To: (name of insurance company)

You are requested and authorized, on a continuing basis, to furnish to (your name) such forms and information as he may request from time to time in connection with my policies in your company. This authorization shall remain in effect until revoked in writing by the undersigned.

Policy-numbers:
_____

Client name:
_____

Client signature:
_____

You can use this idea to sell more insurance on the client, his spouse, children, or to purchase disability income insurance.

On more than one occasion, I had clients paying the annual premiums on the new policies before we got around to withdrawing the dividends. I would go back to them with this idea again and get another sale. One client did this three times.

Conversion of Term Insurance

Earlier I recommended that you do not get into an argument about term insurance versus permanent insurance. Sell all the term insurance that you can. I would be happy to put $10,000,000 of new term insurance on the books each year. The real sale is to convert the term insurance to permanent insurance. The difference now is that you are in a position of advisor to your client. **You talk differently to a client than to a prospect.**

Converting term involves conveying the concepts and showing the numbers.

My presentation book (My Bear Gun) had pages dedicated to showing the wisdom of lifetime coverage and tax deferred cash values. One page showed how term insurance was like car insurance; you paid the premium and hoped you did not have a claim. Every time the term period is renewed, the cost is much higher. At the end of the term period, all premiums were lost. Then as you get old and close to life expectancy, the term insurance is no longer available. One study by Penn State University showed that only 2 percent of all term insurance results in a death claim. **Term insurance**

is actuarially calculated to die before you do. In the beginning, the self-destruct nature of the product is overshadowed by a low premium.

Another page explained that permanent insurance is designed to guarantee to pay off when you die. 100 percent of permanent insurance will result in a claim at death or for the cash values. The cash values of the permanent insurance policy are the reserves that the insurance company is building up to eventually pay this claim. These reserves build up without incurring current income taxes. The policy may include dividends. Policies with dividends have a disappearing feature also. It is the premium that disappears, not the coverage. Interest rates may change with prevailing market interest rates.

However, a permanent insurance policy has a guaranteed cash value and a guaranteed minimum interest rate. Cash values can be borrowed out if needed without incurring income taxes.

If you add a waiver of premium rider and later become totally disabled, the insurance company will waive the premiums due during the disability benefit period (usually to age sixty-five) and may continue to grow the cash values as if you were still making premium payments. This is true for whole life and may be true for universal life if you chose the appropriate waiver of premium rider.

I recommend that you design your pages to hit these key points. Look for additional pages to add. I found helpful articles in *Medical Economics, Fortune, Wall Street Journal, Advisors,* etc.

Another page showed a simple mortality table. I would ask the client to vote upon his own perception of his expectation of life. Then I had printed:

Doesn't It Make Sense to Program Your Life Insurance to Live as Long as You Do?

When you got married you made a commitment. Remember the part that went something like this, "...in sickness and in health, for better or for worse, AS LONG AS WE BOTH SHALL LIVE?"

Did you call a time out and ask to exclude the lifetime stuff? (No)

Then you must want your life insurance to live as long as you do.

In developing numbers for the term conversion, get an illustration of the proposed permanent insurance policy. Subtract from the permanent insurance premium the premium of the term insurance. This difference is your marginal increase in premium. If the term insurance expires in ten or twenty years, show the new rates for the next ten or twenty years until you reach life expectancy. Then compare the marginal increase in premiums versus the increasing cash values.

I like to show the year by year comparison of the marginal increase in premium to the increase in cash value that year. Then I show the total additional premiums paid at ten, twenty, and thirty years to the total cash values at ten, twenty and thirty years.

I also like to show drawing an annual income from the cash values for twenty years after retirement. By using the surrender of cash values up to the basis in the policy and then loans thereafter, I can show a tax-free income in retirement. The policy remains in force until death to avoid taxes on the cash values. Compare the total tax-free income in retirement to the total premiums paid. The last one I ran showed a return of income equal to three times premiums paid.

If you work with the numbers, you should find the best way to illustrate the numbers to convince him that converting to permanent insurance is the logical way to go. **Selling is telling the truth in an attractive and convincing manner.** Here are some phone scripts to use:

- *"As you know, you have a term insurance policy with XYZ company. Term insurance is like renting. Now you can exercise an option to build up equity for yourself. When can we get together to review your option?" (Term conversion option)*
- *"With term insurance, you have to die to win. XYZ has introduced a program for its term policyholders that allows them to win while they are still alive. I am calling to set an appointment to explain this program to you."*
- *"Sound financial planning says that you should minimize expenses and maximize assets. Does that make sense to you? I want to share with you how you can do that with your life insurance. Is the morning or the afternoon better?"*

Buy Term and Invest the Difference

If you find that you need to have this discussion, then here is some help. The purpose of term life insurance is to cover you for a specific term of time. It could be ten, fifteen, or twenty years. Term insurance is like auto insurance. You pay the premium for coverage. If you do not have a claim, then the premium is gone. Almost all term insurance goes away by age eighty. Most people cannot afford to keep their term insurance during retirement. Consequently, 98 percent of term insurance is not in force when the person dies. The insurance company offers low initial rates for this coverage because they are betting that the policy will no longer be in force when the person dies and they will not have to pay off. **"Do you want your life insurance to die before you do?"**

Permanent life insurance (whole life, universal life, variable life) is designed to last for your lifetime. The premiums are level and do not increase as you get older. Some become paid up at some point. The reserve that the company is building up to pay this guaranteed claim is basically the cash value of the policy. (I do not want to get into a very technical discussion of the intricacies of policies). If the owner of the policy wants to accept the cash value in lieu of waiting for the death benefit, then the company is agreeable.

The insurance company knows for sure that they will pay out either the death benefit or the cash value. The initial premiums are higher than term insurance.

Sound financial sense tells you to maximize assets and minimize expenses. Permanent life insurance with its cash values is an asset. Term life insurance is an expense.

Over the last one hundred years, the philosophy of "buy term and invest the difference" has been touted usually by those wanting to sell the difference. We have seen this over and over again.

It changes from time to time as to what to invest in such as gold, mutual funds, real estate, stocks, silver, oil, cyber coins, etc. If it really works, then why don't people rent their home and invest the difference? Why don't people lease cars and invest the difference?

In reality, most prospects who use this excuse cannot afford permanent insurance and do not invest the difference. They spend the difference.

The real questions to ask them are: will you actually save the difference consistently every month; will you actually invest the money; and, will you leave it invested?

One very successful agent in Arizona ran an ad in the local newspaper every day for twenty years offering $100 to anyone who could show that they actually did invest the difference. He had *no* takers in twenty years!

Permanent insurance has the following advantages:

- Lifetime coverage
- Level premiums
- Flexibility
- Builds cash values
- Tax advantaged growth
- Ability to miss a premium and not lose coverage
- Reasonable returns
- Stable and consistent growth in cash values
- Systematic and disciplined approach to accumulating cash values

Term insurance premiums increase substantially upon renewal of the policy after the initial term. Term insurance terminates. With term life insurance, you have to die to win—the sooner the better.

Ask the prospect who espouses that philosophy: *"How have you done? Have you in fact saved the difference since day 1? How much is in your investment account? Have you left it alone?"* Most people have excuses why they have not started the savings yet. What will they do differently in the future? There will always be more "I wants" and "I needs" than "I have". What is really needed is discipline. My experience has been that people talk about this philosophy but no one has actually become wealthy doing it.

The Tough Decision

As a prospect approaches retirement, he begins to think about how much income will be provided after his paychecks stop. If he is a participant in an employer sponsored retirement plan, then at retirement he will have to make a decision on which payout option to take. Retirement plans offer a variety of options: a life income which ends at the prospect's death, a joint and survivor life income which continues the income until both spouses are deceased, and variations of these two. Because the payout period is much longer with two lifetimes instead of one, the payout amount is lower for the joint and survivor option than the life income for the prospect only.

Married prospects most often default to the joint and survivor option. However, there may be a better option. If the prospect chose the life income for himself, he would have a larger income. Then he could buy life insurance with some of this increased income to assure that upon his death, his spouse will have enough money to replace the lost retirement income. If his spouse dies first, the prospect could cash in the life insurance for its cash values, stop paying premiums and continue to have the higher income for the rest of his life.

If you could share this concept with someone who has several years before retirement, the life insurance premium would be lower due to his younger age at purchase. In addition, the policy could be building cash values and dividends that may lower his cost in his retirement years.

"Mr. Prospect, when you retire you will face two major events in your life. The first is that your salary check will change to a retirement payment that may be 50-60 percent of your paycheck. The second event is that you will be faced with a tough decision, whether or not to disinherit the partner you are walking through life with. Choosing a payout option that provides an income to your partner after you die will mean that your retirement check will be even smaller. If I could show you a better way to handle this tough decision, would you be interested?"

This idea will open the prospect's mind to problems and options that he has never considered. He will be anxious for you to do what you can to help him. It also opens the door to discuss how much life insurance he should carry in retirement for other needs.

Conference Table Approach Talk

"Mr. Prospect, I have asked for this appointment because I appreciate the value of your time. I have no reason to believe that you are in the market for life insurance today; however, I have an idea which many successful people in our area have found to be of real value to them. It will only take a few minutes of your time for you to determine whether it has merit for you.

In order to help you make this decision, I would like to ask you four questions. Is that agreeable?

Do you know the amount of capital required for your family to maintain its present or an acceptable standard of living if you had died last night?

Assuming you did not die but became totally disabled, do you have any idea of how much income you and your family would require to maintain your present standard of living and from what sources these funds would be derived?

Do you know the amount of capital which would be required to provide a comfortable retirement for you and your spouse, after the children are educated and the existing mortgages are paid?

Are you aware of the benefits which are available to you and your family from your company retirement plan and Social Security?

You are obviously a busy person and like other successful busy people, you do not have the time to become an expert in every field. You have a staff of *experts who you rely on to advise you.*

This circle represents your personal conference table and let's put you here at the head. (Write prospect's initials at the top center and place an X on the circle). If you have a legal problem, you consult your attorney who sits here (indicated by an X on the circle) and his initials are? If you have a medical problem, you turn to your family physician who is represented here (another X) and his initials are? The same would be true for a tax or accounting problem and his initials are?

Now, how many life insurance policies have you purchased during your lifetime? (Put an X under the circle for each policy). How many of these did you purchase from the same person? Obviously, no one has qualified for this seat at your conference table. This is the job I am applying for. **If you will give me 10% of your confidence, I will earn the other 90%!**

If you like what you have heard so far, I would like to begin by assisting you in measuring your present program with your own objectives. Whether you purchase insurance today or tomorrow is not the matter of greatest importance to me because if I have done an adequate and professional job for you, the next time you need insurance you will call me and not hesitate to recommend me to your friends.

Have you got a few more minutes now to give me the initial information I will need to begin, or would you prefer I come back tomorrow?"

College Education Funding

"One of the finest gifts that you can give your children is a college education. It cannot be lost, rusted or stolen. It will mean tens of thousands of dollars more income than without a college degree. Unfortunately, college is very expensive and many who graduate end up with very large college loans. The solution is for you to set aside money now for that need.

Where you put the money to work should provide good returns, perhaps some guarantees, allow you to be free of current income taxes, and liquid. My recommendation is for you to purchase a cash value building life insurance policy. The cash values will earn guaranteed minimum interest, have a guaranteed minimum cash value and the opportunity to earn more interest or dividends, be tax deferred and be very liquid.

In addition, this policy on you will guarantee that if you do not live to fund this education program, the life insurance proceeds will fully fund their educations on a tax-free basis. If you should become totally disabled during the premium paying period, the insurance company will cover the premiums for you and the cash values will grow at the same rate as if you were paying the premiums.

Isn't this the finest method of funding college educations that you have seen? How much do you want to build up for educations?"

Special Needs Children

Parents of special needs children realize the incredible amount of time, energy, and resources needed to care for these children. One of the worries they have is how to provide this care after they are deceased. The life expectancy of a Down Syndrome (DS) child is age sixty. If the parents are in their 40s, then it is likely that the child will outlive the parents. These parents want their other children to marry and have families of their own.

They do not want to burden the siblings with having to care for the special needs sibling for the rest of his life.

I received a referral to a family of five. At our first meeting, I met Sara, a very loving and sweet girl with DS. The parents were very concerned about her long-term care in the event of their deaths. As long as one of the parents was alive, Sara would be taken care of by a parent. The parents had two other children. The parents wanted the other children to always be there to give Sara love but not to worry that they would have to have her live with them.

I recommended that they purchase a second to die joint life insurance policy of $2,000,000. A second to die policy insures two people (the husband and the wife) and pays the insurance benefit when both insured's have died. This policy has lower premiums than a policy on either the husband or the wife. The $2,000,000 invested should be able to produce a payout of 5 percent a year for the remainder of Sara's life. This would mean about $100,000 a year could be used for Sara's care in a home for special needs adults. To pay the premium, I recommended that they use the Supplemental Security Income (SSI) that they received on her behalf.

To make sure that Sara did not lose valuable government benefits such as SSI, health insurance, and other benefits, the proceeds would be paid to a Special Needs Trust with sprinkling provisions for the benefit of Sara. I referred the parents to an attorney who specializes in Special Needs Trusts. The attorney was so impressed with the funding solution that I provided that she subsequently referred several other families with special needs children to me.

If you run into this situation, talk to an attorney that specializes in Special Needs Trusts. Share your idea of funding the trust with a second to die joint life insurance policy. You will be referred to other families who have the worries that only you can solve.

BUSINESS INSURANCE

How Do You Find Business Owners?

Finding business owner prospects is very similar to prospecting for individuals. The best source is referrals from your existing clients, friends or relatives. The key is to ask: *"Who do you know that owns their own business?"*

The people you do business with are naturals for your approach. When you pay them, say: *"I would appreciate the courtesy of a few minutes of your time to share with you the type of work that I do for my clients. Is now a good time or shall we meet tomorrow?"*

These businesses include your dentist, doctor, repair persons, clothing store, cleaners, restaurant owners, pest control, alarm company, etc.

If you have friends that are small business owners, they can often refer you to their competitors, suppliers, or other companies that they use. Business owners know other business owners.

I utilized this with veterinarians. After making one vet my client, I developed him into a center of influence with other veterinarians. It became quite a nest of clients. Any time a new vet came to town, I knew about him within days of arrival and many of my clients were letting him know that he would be hearing from me soon.

You can also use the business next door approach in business parks, strip centers, and office buildings. With these, you will emphasize that you were sharing some interesting and tax effective ideas with another business in this area and would like to make an appointment to share them with the owner of this business. At least you would like to call them back in ninety days.

Previously I covered the idea of joining an association and prospecting the members. This works well in the business market.

How To Approach The Business Owner; What to Say Or Show

With referrals, ask right then for an appointment. ness insurance specialists. *"We are business insurance specialists. We make sure that our clients are properly covered, with cost effective plans, saving money. Do you have any objections to reviewing your business insurance program with me?"* If you get turned down, then ask to put them on your ninety day call back list.

You could also send out the referral letter or email I described previously. The wording in the letter or email would change to "other business owners". When you call, ask for an appointment. If you are asked what you do, then respond: *"We are business strategies specialists. We help business owners improve their bottom line; attract, retain, and reward key people; and develop benefit plans. When is the best time to get together, Monday or Tuesday?"*

Ask the business owner, *"Have you ever seen The Benefit Stages of a Business chart?"* Pull out the chart and go over it with him. Ask him to check off those benefits that he has already implemented. Then ask for a time to go over the ones he has not done yet.

If you are making cold calls on a business, here is what you can say: *"I happen to be in the area to meet with a business. I am a specialist in business* insurance plans. Have you ever seen the chart *The Benefit Stages of a Business?*" If he says yes, continue with, "Have you enacted all the plans? Let's go over it. Will you please prioritize the plans for me?"

If you are calling on the prospect on the phone, here is what you could say:

"Is it worth fifteen minutes of your time to learn how many of our business owner clients have reduced taxes, retained key people, and improved profits?"

(Reduce taxes through the implementation of a tax-deductible retirement plan.)

Ask Disturbing Questions

- *Mr. Business Owner, if you had died last night, how would these questions be answered today?*
- *Who is running the business?*
- *How does your spouse get income?*
- *Who will pay the creditors?*

- *Does the bank have your personal guarantees?*
- *Are there partners?*
- *What will they want?*
- *Should your share be sold?*
- *Will your partner(s) buy?*
- *At what price?*
- *Is this what you want to happen?*
- *Is your business your biggest asset?*
- *What have you done to protect it from your death or disability?*
- *Do you insure your most valuable business assets...your people?*
- *Do you have a business will?*
- *Are you personally liable for business debts?*
- *Did you sign the loan papers once or twice?*
- *Have you heard of an endorsement or guarantee fee?*
- *Are you interested in reducing taxes?*

Sometimes you can make more money from reducing taxes than from making more money.

Handling Objections

The type of objections in the business market are similar to the personal market.

> **No Money:** *"It is premature of us to be talking of cash outlay until we know if something is needed, how much, and why. Many of our clients find that the tax savings they realize from our planning covers a lot of needs."*
>
> **Too Busy/No Hurry:** *"I can appreciate that many demands are made on your time, as is true of me. This is why I want to set an appointment so we can focus on the important and urgent and not let the urgent but unimportant steal your time. The busier our clients are, the more they need our guidance."*
>
> **Not Interested/No Need:** *"I do not fault you for feeling that way. It is difficult for someone to run his business, keep it profitable, and keep up with all the potential problems that we handle for them. It will only take a few minutes to find out where we might help you."*
>
> **Already Have An Agent**: *"Who is your agent? (pause) No one has an exclusive on all the ideas

that a business might use. I am sure your agent will not mind your reviewing some of those ideas with me."

What's Next?

When you are new to the business market, I recommend that you team up with a successful agent who has made numerous business sales. Preferably that person has the CLU designation.

People want to know that you care about them, more than they care what you know. Your job is to make sure that they know you care.

Confirm to the prospect that you have answers for these disturbing questions and many others. Together you and the CLU have the experience, knowledge, and expertise to give the prospect good input. Let the prospect know that as a team, you have worked with many businesses.

Ask the prospect to provide the following information:

- Business financial statement
- Business tax return

- Personal financial statement
- Personal tax return
- Employee census
- Profit & Loss Statement
- Current benefit plans information
- Projections of future revenues
- Type of business entity
- Ownership
- Estimate of business value

Then schedule an appointment to pick up this information. Once you get all or most of this information, you and your experienced partner will find many ways to help.

BUSINESS INSURANCE SALES IDEAS AND PRESENTATIONS

Benefit Stages of a Business

Create this chart for distribution to business insurance prospects and clients. It will open cases with prospects and give you a guide to follow in developing additional sales to existing clients who still have benefits to provide.

You may want to do this in color. Some of the programs mentioned may be new to you. Research them so you can be conversant on each topic. You want the prospect to know that you know, but remember that you are not there to educate the prospect yet. You want to prepare the presentation first.

Benefit Stages of a Business

Beginning	Growth	Maturity
Buy sell life	Phantom stock	Pension plan
Disability buy sell	Split Dollar Plan	Deferred Comp
Key person life	401(k) plan	Golden Parachute
Guarantee fee	Golden Handcuffs	Estate Planning
SIMPLE Plan	Profit Sharing	Board Comp Plan
		Executive Comp

"Mr. Business Owner, what stage is your business in? Have you instituted all the benefit plans in the beginning stage? How about the growth stage? Let's talk about the next benefit to add."

Buy-Sell or Business Continuation

Here is the written presentation that I used:

It is easier to go into business with someone than to get out. When a co-owner dies or becomes permanently disabled, there is inevitably a business reorganization. The surviving co-owner finds himself in business with the deceased or disabled owner's spouse or heirs.

The surviving co-owner must do one of the following:

- Buy out the heirs.
- Sell out to the heirs.
- Accept the heirs as co-owners and share the decisions and profits.
- Accept outside purchasers if the heirs sell their interests.

Without a specified price or funding in place, the surviving owner may not be in a good position to buy out the heirs. Selling to the heirs may not get the surviving owner a good price and the surviving owner would lose his income. New owners may not share the same philosophy or business style. They could be disruptive to the business. The surviving owner's business value could be at risk due to the new owners' incompetency.

Likewise, the heirs could be dependent on the surviving owner for financial support. Will the business be profitable enough to pay the surviving owner and pay dividends to the heirs? Will the heirs be expected to sign for business loans? Will they be comfortable that the surviving owner will preserve and enhance their business assets? You may not want your heirs to be dependent on the surviving owner's skills to keep the business successful.

The odds that one of two business owners will die before age sixty-five vary according to the ages of the owners at the time. The range is from 20 to 40 percent. When you add the odds that one owner could become permanently disabled before age sixty-five, the odds of needing a buyout agreement increase substantially. To deny the importance of addressing the issue of business continuation is very risky for any business owner.

The solution is the establishment of a funded business buy sell agreement. This agreement is a legal document which requires the business or the surviving owner to buy the interest of the deceased, retiring or permanently disabled owner.

It requires the heirs or disabled partner to sell the interest at an agreed upon price. It spells out the buy-out price and pay-off terms. The amounts paid for a person's interest in a business in the event of a death or a permanent disability may be higher than at retirement or withdrawal, since a retiring or withdrawing owner could become a competitor someday.

The advantages of a properly arranged buy-sell agreement include:

- No dispute about price or terms.
- A smooth transition of ownership and control.
- Heirs are assured of the value of their interest.
- Heirs are not tied to the business.

- Surviving owner avoids interference from heirs or other purchasers in running the business.
- Heirs have cash to pay estate taxes without liquidating other assets.
- Disputes are minimized.

A buy-sell agreement is only as good as its funding. There are four ways to fund a buy-sell agreement: cash, borrowing, installment payments, and insurance.

- Cash: Most businesses do not keep substantial amounts of cash around to fund buy-sell agreements. They use cash in the business or pay it out to the owners. Too much cash in the business may be subject to a retained earnings tax.
- Borrowing: Following the death of a key owner, it may be difficult for the surviving owner to borrow money from a financial institution, especially when it is used to finance buying out an owner and not buying more assets. This money will have

to be paid back with after tax earnings plus interest. This creates a big liability for the future of the company.

- Installment payments: This puts the heirs in the position of being the lender. The payments are a drain on the future income of the company. Most of the payments will be non-deductible. If the surviving owner defaults, the heirs will lose out.

- Insurance: The most cost-effective method to guarantee the funding is to purchase life insurance on each owner and disability buy-out insurance, if available. With a manageable premium, you are able to collect the proceeds in tax-free cash when needed most. The proper type of life insurance can also serve a double duty. It can build a tax deferred "sinking fund" that can be used to help fund a retirement or withdrawal buy-out. The amount of insurance could be for an amount larger than the current buy-out price. In that way, you have covered some growth avoiding the need to purchase more insurance every year.

A buy-sell arrangement can either be an entity purchase or cross purchase plan. In an entity purchase plan, the business enters into an agreement with each owner to buy their interest. The advantages of this plan are that the business pays the premiums for the insurance and the business buys one policy per owner.

In a cross-purchase plan, the owners enter into an agreement with each other. The advantages of this plan are that upon buying out an owner, the surviving owner or owners get a resulting step-up basis for tax purposes and the insurance proceeds are not subject to the claims of business creditors. If there are more than two owners, the number of policies increases substantially. For example, a cross purchase buy-sell for three owners would require six policies; four owners require twelve policies.

A third alternative is to have a trusteed cross purchase plan. A trust is created by the owners. The trust will buy out the interest of a deceased, disabled or withdrawing owner. The trust will own a policy on each owner. After purchasing an interest, the trust will distribute it proportionally to the surviving owners. In this method, only one policy is purchased per owner and the surviving owners get a stepped-up basis. We will handle the funding details and assist your attorney with implementing the agreement.

This is the most basic of life insurance needs for a business. The owners put their money, time, and energy into the business to make it a success. All could be lost quickly if provision is not made for the continuation of the business upon an owner's death or long-term disability. The best time to make an exit plan is not when you are about to exit. It is when you enter the business.

This is especially true for sole proprietorships. This business is dependent on one owner. There are no partners or co-shareholders to buy the owner out. In this case, I have used key employees or competitors to set up a buy sell arrangement.

If the business has a key employee, it is a natural to set up a buy-sell agreement between the owner and the key employee. Using life insurance and disability buy-out insurance is necessary since most key employees do not have the resources to start their own business or buy an existing one. In this way, the key employee has an opportunity someday to perhaps own a successful business and he is even more committed to the success of the business. The owner has locked in a future buyer if he dies prematurely, and his heirs will be paid in tax free cash.

If the key person leaves, the buy-sell agreement requires that the key person must transfer ownership of the policies back to the business owner.

If the owner of the business has a friendly competitor in the area, then he could enter into a buy-sell agreement with his competitor. Most often, the competitor is a sole proprietor who also needs a guaranteed buyer of his business if he were to die prematurely.

I have used this with veterinarians, dentists, physicians, and other small businesses. It can work for the independent dry cleaner, hardware store, etc.

Once the buy-sell insurance is in force, stay in touch with the owner. Some businesses will grow in value resulting in more sales to increase the coverage needed and perhaps more like to owners to insure.

"Mr. Jones, if your associate, Mr. Smith, were to die, would you like to own the entire business? (answer is usually yes)

"Do you have the necessary $250,000 with which to buy the ownership interest owned by Mr. Smith?"

(answer is usually no)

"Suppose you were given twenty years in which to raise the $ 250,000, could you do it? (usual answer is yes) *"This means that you will have to set aside $12,500 a year for the next twenty years, ignoring interest for the moment."*

The unfortunate part of setting aside the $ 12,500 a year is that should Mr. Smith die a year or two from now, all you will have towards the $250,000 will be $12,500 or $25,000. I have a perfect solution to your problem.

With this series of questions, you have established: that Mr. Jones wants to buy the business if Mr. Smith dies, that Mr. Jones does not have the $250,000 needed, and that Mr. Jones has committed himself to spending $12,500 a year to solve this problem. You will then show him a permanent policy for $250,000 that has a premium less than $12,500 a year and will build cash values.

In twenty years, the policy's cash values should be greater than the premiums paid.

Key Person Insurance

The assets of a business that have the highest value are the key people. They can turn fixed assets into profits. The problems created by the death or long-term disability of a key person are:

- creditors look for payment
- new money sources adopt a wait and see policy
- customers lose confidence
- competitors take immediate advantage of lost momentum
- employees start looking for another position

A key person can be the person in charge of financial matters, the production manager, the sales director or salesperson, or the person with unique skills that would be hard to replace.

The solution is to have key person life insurance and disability insurance in place. These coverages will provide:

- cash to keep the company operating
- cash to assure creditors their loans are safe
- cash to assure customers and employees the company will continue to operate
- cash to demonstrate to shareholders the foresight, capacity, and character of company management

The company will be the owner and beneficiary of these policies. If a key person leaves, the company can either cash in the policies or transfer them to insure another key person.

Loan Guarantee Fee

Here is my written presentation:

When a privately owned business borrows money from a financial institution, the lender requires the business owner to sign the loan document twice:

first, as the officer of the business, and second, personally guaranteeing the payment of the loan.

This personal guarantee obligates the business owner's personal assets as collateral for the loan. In the event of the business owner's death, the lender could look to the business owner's house, savings, and investments to repay the loan. The owner's spouse is usually also obligated for the loan.

Many business owners charge the business a Loan Guarantee Fee of 1 percent of the loan per year. This fee is used to pay premiums on a life insurance policy on the business owner's life equal to the original loan amount. This policy is owned by the business owner personally. The beneficiary is the owner's spouse. Upon death, the spouse receives the life insurance proceeds income tax free.

If the lender calls in the loan upon the owner's death, the spouse can loan the insurance proceeds to the business to pay off the remaining loan balance. Later, when the business makes profits or is sold, the business can repay the loan to the spouse. The spouse receives these funds income tax free.

Phantom Stock Plan

The purposes of a phantom stock plan are: to reward executives who have a major influence on the success of the business; to attract, retain, and motivate top management; and to not dilute ownership of the company. Also, the company does not have to disclose company finances to the employee as it would to an actual shareholder.

The solution is that the company would grant "phantom" units of company stock each year in an amount equal to an agreed upon formula. It is a non-qualified deferred compensation agreement. (Non-qualified means not tax deductible.) At retirement, the company will pay out to the participant an amount equal to the appreciated value of the units credited to his account.

The advantages to the company are: it fosters a shareholder mentality without creating more shareholders; attracts, retains, and motivates key employees; is flexible and selective; and is easy to administer. The advantages to the employee are: he can share in the company's success, benefit is tax deferred until payment is received, and it provides a sense of job security.

Here is how it works. Periodically the employee will have phantom stock units awarded to his account. The basis of the phantom stock unit will be the book value of a share of stock at the time of the award. The employee must remain with the company for a specified number of years or forfeit the benefit. The benefit is paid out in the event of the employee's premature death. At retirement or termination of employment after the specified number of years, the employee will receive a payment equal to the appreciation in the phantom stock units from the date of grant to the date of distribution. Payment can be made in a lump sum or in a fixed number of installments.

Life insurance is purchased by the company on the employee to cover the anticipated potential payout in the event of a premature death and to build cash values for the expected payout at retirement.

Here is how I described the phantom stock plan in my presentations:

A Growth Participation Plan is a plan that allows an employee, who is interested in having an ownership interest in the company, to participate in the growth of the company without you actually giving up ownership. This is utilized especially when the key person expresses a strong interest in ownership or is a candidate as a future purchaser of the business.

Split-Dollar Plans

Split-dollar is a method of paying premiums on a life insurance policy. An employer and employee agree to "split" both the cost (premiums) and the benefits (cash values and death benefits) of a permanent life insurance policy.

The two basic forms of policy ownership for split-dollar are:

Endorsement method: The employer owns the policy, but a written endorsement is added to the policy which splits the benefits between the employer and the employee.

Collateral assignment method: The employee owns the policy and assigns certain interests in the policy to the employer as collateral for payments made by the employer. (This is the one I prefer.)

The premium can be split either where the employer pays an amount equal to annual cash value buildup and the employee pays the rest of the premium, or the employer pays the entire premium and the employee is taxed on the value of the economic benefit received. The second option is the one I have used.

The benefits are usually split where the employer gets a return of the premiums paid by the employer and the employee gets the balance of the proceeds.

This is a real benefit for the employee to be able to own the life insurance desired and not struggle with the premium. For the employer, it is an attractive benefit to attract and retain key employees. It is also a way that an employee can afford life insurance to fund a cross purchase buy-sell agreement.

The real benefit for the employer is that the employee is tied into the employer more and the employer's investment is usually covered by the cash values of the policy. The cost to the employer is the loss of interest that these premiums could have earned.

Golden Handcuffs Executive Compensation

Here is my written presentation:

One area often overlooked by employers is that of incentive compensation for key employees. Most often employers use bonuses, whether monthly, quarterly, or annually, to motivate superior performance from their key employees. One disadvantage of bonuses is the discounted value perceived by the employees due to taxes, particularly bonuses of less frequency. There is a tendency by employees to focus on the net check after taxes rather the full amount of the bonus.

Another disadvantage with the typical bonus-based incentive system is that the bonuses soon are perceived as entitlements and are expected every year.

Some far-sighted employers have implemented incentive-based compensation plans in addition to bonus-based incentive systems. These plans are numerous and vary in specific approaches.

They have several key components: (1) the bonuses are earned by the key employees over time and given at some designated point in the future, which is determined by the employer; (2) the bonuses are significant enough to motivate employees despite having to wait; and (3) the bonuses are subject to vesting periods determined by the employer.

The intent is to retain key employees and keep them motivated.

The following describe several different plans:

Defined Benefit Golden Handcuffs, Incentive Driven Golden Handcuffs, and Leveraged Bonus Plans.

- Defined Benefit Golden Handcuffs is a program that provides a pre-defined retirement benefit for select key employees. The funding is fixed. It can have a long vesting schedule (for example, ten or fifteen years).
- Incentive Driven Golden Handcuffs is the same as the Defined Benefit plan except that the funding is based upon a percentage of compensation as determined by their performance. The benefit is based on the investment results of the funding.

- Leveraged Bonus Plan is a plan that puts the bonus in a tax deferred life insurance policy owned by the key employee but restricts access to the cash values for a predetermined number of years or until the employer releases the restriction. This is also known as a Section 162 Bonus Plan.

I have used these concepts quite a lot. Once the employer started a plan for one employee, usually he would add others to the plan over time. One client set this up for ten employees. It always results in a permanent life insurance sale. Often there would be a disability income insurance sale as well.

When describing the benefits to the employee, I state the employer has put $XXX in escrow for his future benefit in the event of his premature death, retirement at age sixty-five, or disability.

One day, a client called me and asked that I come by his office. When we met, he explained that his most important employee had been offered a large raise to switch to his competitor. Before agreeing to switch, the employee requested that the competitor put a sum equal to the Golden

Handcuffs benefit in escrow for him as his present employer had done. The competitor refused to do that, so the employee stayed with my client. My client wanted to implement six more plans immediately for other key employees.

How does it work? The employer purchases a permanent life insurance policy and disability income insurance policy on the employee with the employer as owner and beneficiary. An agreement is signed defining the benefits to the employee. If the employee dies prematurely, the insurance will be enough to pay the promised benefit which is a monthly income for a stated number of years. The employer will get a tax deduction for the insurance proceeds paid out and earn some interest on the proceeds waiting to be paid out.

At retirement, the employer will use the cash values to pay the monthly benefit over a stated number of years. The employer has the added leverage of the tax savings from tax deducting these payments. The employer will also earn interest on the cash values not yet used. The combination of cash values, tax savings, and interest are enough to pay the retirement benefit where the cash values alone may not be enough.

The disability income feature depends on the employee's ability to qualify for disability insurance benefits. Because the degree of disability must be considered, some employers choose not to include disability. I personally like it included.

An example of my presentation will illustrate how the plan is described to the employee on page 1, and page 2 is given to the employer to describe the benefits and cost. I will use an actual case as an example but with names removed.

(Page 1)

A SELECTIVE EXECUTIVE BENEFIT PLAN For G...

The purpose of this non-qualified defined benefit plan is to thank you for your past service to K... Construction and to encourage you to remain a committed key member of the company.

Maximum Benefit: $500,000

Plan Benefit Schedule and Features:

- If you die while employed by K... Construction, your chosen beneficiary will receive an income of **$50,000 a year for ten years.**

- When you retire (after age sixty-five), you will receive an income of **$50,000 a year for ten years.**
- If you become totally disabled as defined by the insurance company, you will receive a benefit of **$50,000 a year for ten years** or until your recovery, whichever comes first.
- You will become vested in the accrued pro-rata retirement benefits of the Plan, payable at age sixty-five, according to the following schedule: 100 percent vested after ten more years of service with the company.

These unique benefits are provided at no cost to you by the company.

(Page 2)

A SELECTIVE EXECUTIVE BENEFIT PLAN For G...

The purpose of this non-qualified defined benefit plan is to reward G... for his past service and to retain him for the future. It provides **$50,000 a year for ten years** in the event of his death, total disability, or his retirement after age sixty-five.

Maximum Benefit: $500,000

Features:

- The insurance policies are owned by the company.
- The cash values of the policy are an asset of the company and available to the company, if needed.
- The benefits are tax deductible by the company as they are paid to the employee or beneficiary. Therefore, the cost to the company is reduced by the taxes saved.
- The proceeds from the insurance policy will be received by the company tax-free.
- The company will be able to earn interest on the proceeds during the payout period.
- The Plan is selective, and the company can set it up for any key employee with any level of benefits.
- The monthly cost for the insurance policies is $512.86.

- The Plan could provide some cost recovery for the company.

You can see that the presentation is simple to explain to the employee and easy for the employer to understand. The premiums obviously vary by age and insurability. You can get quite creative in designing the benefit amounts and payment periods. I used as a rule of thumb that I wanted the total benefit to be five times the employee's annual income.

If you were to do an incentive driven plan, you would define the minimum premium that would go into the insurance policy, and then allow additional amounts to be paid into the policy based upon the employee achieving certain standards of performance. You would have to use a flexible premium policy. This is a much more complicated plan to administer. The benefit will be determined at retirement based on how much the cash values had been built up.

A Section 162 Bonus Plan is a life insurance policy owned by the employee with the employer paying the premium. There is a restrictive endorsement added to the policy that states that for a certain number of years the employer must approve any withdrawals of cash values. The premium is considered a bonus to the employee and the employee pays the tax on the bonus. It is better as the employee to pay the tax on the premium than the actual premium.

Tax Saving Ideas

I had several people ask me what tax saving ideas we could offer a business. Here are a few:

- Retirement plan: This could be a SIMPLE IRA, 401(k) plan, profit sharing or pension plan. I have worked closely with a local retirement plan administration company to be able to show retirement plan options to clients.
- HRA or HSA accounts: This gives the employer and employees an opportunity to have eligible medical, dental, and vision expenses paid with pre-tax dollars.
- State tax credits: Some states provide that certain donations to charities are eligible

for credits against your state taxes.
- Business expenses: You may find that there are potential business expenses that are being paid with personal dollars. This is especially true if the client is conducting business activities at home. These expenses could include business related entertainment, cell phone cost, computer and internet expenses, etc.
- FICA costs: One client I had was earning above the maximum income for FICA payments. He was also paying a much smaller salary to his spouse. At retirement, his spouse would get a much higher Social Security benefit as the owner's spouse than she would get from her own Social Security. Therefore, it was a waste of money to pay FICA on her behalf. Not paying her a salary at all saved them 15.6 percent FICA taxes on the money that was being paid to her. That saved them $7,500 in FICA taxes annually.

There may be more ways to help clients save taxes. This subject is worth learning more about with the aid of experienced financial planners and CPAs.

CREATING AND SUSTAINING A SUCCESSFUL BUSINESS

In the following section, I will share ideas and activities necessary to build and sustain your success in the life insurance business. I want to emphasize that there are no shortcuts to doing the right things right. You must put forth the energy, discipline, and character to make yourself into a professional.

If you were studying to be a physician, you would have years of study and internships before you could begin practicing. Likewise, you must have the same dedication to years of study, hard work, and consistency to become a success.

Education

I mentioned it earlier. You must be a student of this business. You will need to *read* about the products you sell, concepts like buy sell, businesses, taxes, and selling skills. You need to *attend* conferences and meetings for the purpose of picking up new ideas and ways to better communicate with your prospects and clients. You will need to *practice* how and what you will say to prospects and clients. **Ad Lib is for Amateurs.**

The time you spend practicing will not be wasted if it makes you better. **If your goal is to chop down the forest, you are not losing time by sharpening your axe.**

I read that it takes ten thousand hours of practice to be an expert in a field. The Beatles spent that much time playing before they "exploded" on the music scene. Professional athletes did the same before they became professionals. A violin virtuoso takes ten thousand hours of practice to be the best. The truly greats in the life insurance business can look back at more than ten thousand hours of study, practice, and experience. Will you? Do you have the drive to commit yourself that fully to becoming a success in this business? For those who do, the rewards are tremendous for the rest of their lives.

You will want to commit yourself to getting your CLU as soon as you can. I would often say to prospects and clients that "*I am on schedule to becoming a CLU.*" Then I would show them a brochure from The American College that explained what CLU is. I gave out lots of those brochures. Many clients at annual reviews would ask me how I was doing on getting my CLU. That was motivation.

Once you get your CLU, then press on to getting your ChFC and MSFS. The courses are excellent, and you will put that information to good use in your business. Having those designations and a master's degree will put you ahead of 99 percent of all other life insurance agents. **Knowledge is power and confidence.**

Policy Production Goal

Over the years, I found that I could not control the size of the policies I sold. Some were small and some were big. What I could control was the number of policies I sold. This was a result of the number of interviews I had. That number was directly affected by the number of prospects I generated. The one thing I could control was my activity.

I also learned that there was a direct correlation between the number of policies I sold and the income I earned. The key number for success was to sell over one hundred policies a year.

My goal was to have *five hundred* clients. With five hundred clients, you should be able to sell one hundred clients a year additional coverage. This is great for your attitude. It makes you stronger in asking for referrals. It establishes a solid financial foundation for you.

Over time, your average size sale will get larger as your clients age and their incomes get larger. You will sell larger amounts of coverage at higher premiums to your clients. You will also be selling a lot more coverage in the business market.

If I were to identify the single most important measure of your future success, it would be selling one hundred plus policies a year.

The Goal Card

It is not hard to get distracted in this busy life we have. The Goal Card was developed to keep you focused on the most important goals you have. It is a three inch by five-inch card that you constantly carry in your shirt pocket or purse. On one side, you put the title **Goal Card**.

Below that on the left side, you write the amount of first year commissions (FYC) that you want to earn this month.

On the right side, you put the number of policies you want to sell this month to make that happen.

On the back side, you write down your three major goals for the year. These may be business goals or personal goals.

These goals are written as if they have already been done.

Each time you make a sale, you pull out the card.

You draw a line through the first-year commission goal number and subtract the amount you just made. Now you write down the new number. This is what you have left to do this month.

If you reach zero and still have some days in the month left, you change to color ink and start building the number up. Likewise, you cross through the policy number, subtract the number of policies you sold, and you have your number still to go.

Here is what it would look like:

GOAL CARD

FYC	POLICIES
$5,000	12
4,200	11
3,000	9
1,810	6
900	5
100	3

You can see that there were some days with multiple sales. The last entry shows that I completed the commission goal and have $100 more. I still have three more policies to sell this month.

The back side looks like this:

1. I earn $60,000 in FYC.
2. I am out of debt.
3. I am a terrific husband and father.

Obviously, you will change these goals each year. Every day you will pull out the card when you change shirts, or pull out the card to record on it, or while looking for something else in your pocket. When you do, you will see one side or the other. It will be a constant reminder of what your goals are and where you stand that month toward your goals.

Often when I would see an associate in the office or at a meeting, I would ask him to show me his goal card. My associates would also ask to see mine. It kept us accountable for our activities. I urge you to adopt this Goal Card and you too will find that it works!

Time Management

We all have the same amount of time, but it is what you do with your time that dictates your success. You must ask yourself constantly: **Is This the Best Use of My Time Right Now?**

You should start your day early, say 5:15 A.M. Exercise. Get a good breakfast and then go out the door running.

"Every morning in Africa, a gazelle wakes up. It knows it must outrun the fastest lion or it will be killed. Every morning in Africa, a lion wakes up. It knows that it must run faster than the slowest gazelle or it will starve. It doesn't matter whether you're a lion or a gazelle—when the sun comes up, you'd better be running."

Do your prospects get to work before you do?

Fill up each day with appointments. If you have some free time, study or phone or drop in on a client at work (prospecting for fellow employees). Have set times every day for your telephoning.

Put a friendly picture nearby when phoning so that you have a smile in your voice.

Put a thermometer of goals on your bathroom mirror as a daily reminder of where you stand toward your goals.

Use the Goal Card.

Organize your desk to eliminate clutter on top. Paper shuffling is unproductive. File everything. Know the difference between urgent and important. One of the keys to success is focusing on using your time productively.

Remember that the only man that ever got all his work done by Friday was Robinson Crusoe!

Sell with Conviction

Believe in what you are selling. **You must own it to sell it.** Do an analysis of your situation and then buy all that is needed.

This includes the maximum disability income insurance that the insurance company will issue. How can you effectively handle the "I cannot afford it" objection if you personally have not accepted that you must afford it? I had another MDRT member do an analysis of my situation. It resulted in me doubling my coverage and converting a lot of my term insurance to permanent coverage.

Handle objections by sincerely believing *that it is in the prospect's best interest to buy.* Put the problems that the family faces without this coverage squarely on *their* shoulders. You must be a bit of an actor to dramatize in words what could happen to the family if death or totally disability occurs without the needed coverage.

Attitude

Your attitude will determine your altitude. You need to be the most positive and excited person you know. The prospects and clients will pick up on your energy. If you are enthusiastic about the good that you do and have a sincere desire to help people, others will perceive you as a caring person whom they can trust. Your clients will never be more excited than you are. So be excited!

You will face a lot of rejection in the beginning of your career. How you overcome it will predict your future.

When your attitude gets down, take time to write down three things you are very thankful for. That should get you in a positive frame of mind. Call your spouse, a friend or an associate and ask for a cheerleading session.

Persistence: I like these words from former President Calvin Coolidge:

Persistence...

"Nothing in the world can take the place of persistence. Talent will not; nothing is more

common than unsuccessful men with talent. Genius will not; unrewarded genius is almost a proverb. Education will not; the world is full of educated derelicts. Persistence and determination alone are omnipotent."

A FINAL NOTE

This has been a labor of hope and care. I hope that the ideas herein will make your path to success a little easier. I truly care that you succeed.

I welcome your comments and questions at **www.jimvanhouten.com** if it will clarify or add to the value you gain from this Handbook. There is much more that I could have added but I did not want to overwhelm you. Please take seriously what I have shared. It is all field tested and helped make my career a big success. What I enjoyed most in my working life was helping people. Through this Handbook, I hope to keep on doing that.

A friend of mine asked why I took so much time and thought to create this Handbook. The following poem best summarizes my answer.

Building the Bridge for Him

An old man, going on a lone highway,
Came at the evening, cold and gray,
To a chasm, vast and deep and wide,
Through which was flowing a sullen tide.
The old man crossed in the twilight dim –
That sullen stream had no fears for him;
But he turned, when he reached the other side,
And built a bridge to span the tide.

"Old man," said a fellow pilgrim near
"You are wasting strength in building here.
Your journey will end with the ending day;
You will never again must pass this way.
You have crossed the chasm deep and wide,
Why build you a bridge at the eventide?"

The builder lifted his old gray head.

"Good friend, in the path I have come," he said,

"There followeth after me today

A youth whose feet must pass this way.

This chasm that has been naught to me

To that fair-haired youth may a pitfall be.

He, too, must cross in the twilight dim;

Good friend I am building the bridge for him."

About the Author

Jim Van Houten, CLU, ChFC, MSFS, MSM

A native of Arizona, Jim has over 50 years of experience providing financial services. He is the second generation of Van Houtens to work in the industry, providing financial services to clients from all over the nation.

Jim has 5 degrees and designations:

- Bachelor of Science in Finance (1969)
- Chartered Life Underwriter (CLU), advanced degree in life insurance (1971)
- Masters of Science in Financial Services (MSFS) (1979)
- Chartered Financial Consultant (ChFC), an advanced degree in financial consulting (1982)
- Masters of Science in Management (MSM) (1996)

Jim also owned one of the largest financial services firm in Arizona and New Mexico from 1979 to 1997, and was a nationally recognized speaker.

His agency received 2 President's Trophy awards from MassMutual. The President's Trophy means that the agency was rated one of the top five in the nation.

He had over 35 years of qualification in the Million Dollar Round Table (MDRT), an international organization. Jim was a key speaker at the MDRT conference in 1980. Twice he qualified for the exclusive Top of the Table. Jim was Chair of the committee that determined the new qualifications for MDRT based on income rather than volume. This was a difficult task given the differences in monetary standards around the world.

He was the founding Vice Chairman of the joint GAMC/MDRT Mentoring Council. He was a member of Arizona Business Leadership Association and served on its Board for 8 years.

In 2001 Jim co-founded with his son, Jameson, a financial planning and investment management firm.

This firm is a Registered Investment Advisor (RIA) with over $400 million in assets under the firm's management. Jim retired from the firm on August 2, 2013.

His second book, **A Life with Significance: Leaving a Legacy through Charitable Planned Giving**, was released in January, 2020. His third book, **Buying Life Insurance: How to Make an Informed Choice**, was released in October, 2020. His newest book, **Selling Life Insurance: Rising to a Higher Income**, was published in January, 2021.

His community involvements included: Charter Member of Paradise Valley United Methodist Church; member of the University of Arizona President's Club; past Board Member of Barrows Neurological Institute Foundation; past Board Member of the Arizona Friends of Foster Children Foundation; retired Board Member of the Valley of the Sun YMCA after serving 37 years and its President in 1989; retired Board Member of the National Board of the YMCA of the USA serving for 8 years; past Board Member of the Claremont School of Theology; and, past Board Member of the Human Liberty ARTT Foundation. He is currently a member of the University of Arizona Cancer Center Advisory Board.

Jim has been happily married for over 52 years and has three adult sons, two daughters-in-law and five grandchildren. He lost a son in 2020.

He served as a Little League coach for 18 years, on the Little League Board for 12 years, and a Boy Scout leader for 11 years.

He enjoys reading, playing golf, biking and spending his summers in the cool weather of Show Low, AZ.

www.ingramcontent.com/pod-product-compliance
Lightning Source LLC
Chambersburg PA
CBHW071404210526
45465CB00001B/245